The Baptism in the Holy Spirit

the Good, the Bad and the Ugly

By Jerry Carlson

3-21-2021
To my brother
EZEKIEL !
I'm so proud of you
for your walk with Jesus !!!
STAY STRONG!. keep a
spiritual BACKBONE !!!
Never Bow to anyone
or anything EXCEPT to
JESUS !!!.
I Love you Bro!
Jerry
Jer 9=23-24
Psalm 25 =4-5
Phil 3-8-11
Rom 14-8

The Baptism in the Holy Spirit
the Good, the Bad
and the Ugly
by Jerry Carlson

First Edition

All scriptures are quoted from the New King James Version unless otherwise noted

ISBN 978-0-9915811-6-0

Cover Photo by Jerry Carlson
Rogue River, Oregon 2016. A reminder of John 7:38-39.
Back cover photo: Jerry Carlson and his dog Boots.

Contact: jerry.carlson.writer@gmail.com
Printed in the United States of America

INTRODUCTION

I do not see myself as a theologian or a great teacher. I do know that God has been working in and through my life by the power of His Holy Spirit. Christians and those who are baptized in the Holy Spirit and speak in tongues are not perfect. God is still working on all of us. Get ready, in these last days we need the power of the Spirit working in our lives.

The "good" part of the Holy Spirit cannot be contained in books because there is so much that God has done by His Holy Spirit in and through lives. I will provide some testimonies of how God has worked in the lives of people and in my life.

Unfortunately, I'm a perfect example of how something "bad" can result from being baptized in the Holy Spirit and I will share it in detail in that chapter title. I will share some other things that can happen also, which, I trust will be a safeguard for you and for those you may be mentoring.

There have been things that people have said or done that are weird, yet the Holy Spirit seems to get the credit for them. I refer to them in the "ugly" chapter of this book. I believe that these weird things have fueled the fire in the conflict between denominations and relationships over the decades.

In Acts 21:19 Paul had returned from his missionary trip and "reported in detail" all that God had done "through his ministry". Paul was not prideful or bragging; he was just reporting the facts as I will be doing in this book.

Let me assure you that it is definitely not my goal that you will be speaking in tongues when you finish reading this book. Yes, you heard me right! If you've accepted Christ do you wonder where the power is? I pray that you will come to know the person of the Holy Spirit as He pours that power into your life in new ways. Let's dive into the living, breathing Spirit of God together.

ACKNOWLEDGEMENTS

There are so many that have been a major influence in my life. Listening to an old Bible teacher, Bob Mumford, on cassette tapes gave me the greatest foundation and hunger for more of Jesus in the early 1970s. Next is Claude O Wood, who led me into the baptism of the Holy Spirit on February 11, 1973. For that I will be forever grateful. I have also used Oswald Chambers "My Utmost for His Highest" devotional for decades, which has continued to challenge me in walking close to Jesus, and learning to be sensitive to the Holy Spirit.

Thank you Pastor Roger Whitlow, for teaching me how to live a balanced life in the Word and the Spirit. Pastor Tim Howard thanks for showing me how to be real and transparent while walking in the Spirit. Jack Deere, Robert Morris and others have helped me grow in major ways. Pastor John Amstutz, thank you for your teaching and counsel as I continue to pick your brain even as I write this book.

My two sons, Luke and Bart have been such a blessing in my life. Luke was a child after God's own heart and is more mature than me as he would astound us with his God like responses to crisis or other situations as a teenager. Luke was an earthly father pleaser growing up and became a heavenly Father pleaser. The Lord has used Luke to speak into lives, including mine.

Bart is generous and a man of integrity. Oh, how I thank the Lord for Bart who, as a child, questioned my "religious rules" and put me on my knees and in the word of God. The Lord used Bart to set me free from manmade rules and traditions of men as I studied the Bible.

I'm amazed by the talent, skills and gifts God has given to Luke and Bart. The Lord knew I needed those boys in my life and I love them more than they know. I thank the Lord for you Luke and Bart and I am so proud of you.

I want to thank my amazing granddaughter Brianna Carlson for her wisdom and wise counsel in helping me edit this book. Her input has helped me to get rid of the "Christianese" and many terms that are so common in the church today but foreign to many young people. I'm so very proud of you and I love you!

Of course I saved the best for last, my dear wife Barbara and my sister in the Lord! Her counsel, example, correction and direction have been such a blessing and inspiration to me even though most of the time I don't appreciate it at first. Truth is hard to swallow isn't it? I call Barbara "My Angel" as the Lord sent her from heaven for me, a broken vessel. Oh, how I needed her and am so thankful for her! Her wisdom and insight has saved me many times from doing something stupid as she is an amazing woman of God. I have told others that "I thank the Lord that Barbara loves Jesus more than me". To have a Godly spouse is a special treasure on this side of heaven. I love you Angel!

TABLE OF CONTENTS

CHAPTER 1
A PHARISEE OF PHARISEES

In the winter snow of October 1945, I was born in the upper peninsula of Michigan west of Houghton and near the shore of Lake Superior. I was the baby in the family with two brothers, Jim (nicknamed JJ) who was 4 years older and Ralph (Junior) who was 8 years older than me. My family was part of the Apostolic Lutheran Church along with all my relatives on my mother's side. Our church believed in the shed blood of Jesus Christ on the cross for our sins and that Jesus rose again from the dead to give us eternal life when we repent, accepting His offer of salvation. We didn't believe in the baptism of the Holy Spirit or speaking in tongues. We were and they still are a basic Bible believing church who loves the Lord and walks out their faith in this present world.

We moved away when I was about 5 years old and after moving back and forth between New Mexico and Lower Michigan, we ended up in Arizona when I was about 7 years old. By the way, we discovered that my mother was the one who always wanted to move.

There were no Apostolic Lutheran churches in New Mexico or Arizona so my parents started visiting many churches looking for a church that taught the Bible and we ended up in the Assemblies of God (AG) churches.

What was with these "Pentecostals?" They were playing instruments, clapping to the music and raising their hands while praising God. They also prayed at an altar bench in front of the church after the service. We didn't do any of that in the Lutheran church when I was a child. This was a radical change in the way I was raised in church. The Carlson family walked with God with all we knew at that time as I was growing up.

My mother continued to train me in the Lutheran Catechism, memorizing the Apostles Creed, the 10 commandments and

1

more. When I was 16 years old my mom sent me to a two week Confirmation Class in Phoenix. The Apostolic Lutheran church had built a building by this time and a pastor came from Minnesota to teach the class. Interestingly enough I was attending the AG on Wednesday night and weekends and a Lutheran Confirmation Class during the week. Do not get me wrong, I'm so thankful for the training and my mother's persistence in teaching me about the Bible and using the Catechism, that was good for me and it built a foundation.

We were raised in a very strict home and we were told not to attend school sports, bowling, shows or dancing, and basically everything was a sin. We didn't play cards, we had no TV and we didn't play table games with dice. We sure didn't use "swear words" like darn or heck. We felt that we were very holy and set apart from the world.

Whenever I'm teaching, I share that we were so much holier than anyone else because my mother added laws that Moses forgot. To give you two examples, we could not use scissors or clip our fingernails on Sunday. It is interesting that the Pharisees actually wanted to keep the Sabbath day holy, so that is why they added laws to try and prevent people from breaking the Sabbath. I have to commend my mother as her heart was right but she was legalistic.

When I was a young teenager I asked my mom why we could not go bowling. She looked at me and said with a very hard voice, "Because there are sinners there!" Wow, I never questioned her but in my mind I wondered why then did she go to the grocery store, which made no sense to me.

My mother put the literal fear of God in me, so I felt like God was watching me every minute to see if I did anything wrong. It was more than a reverence type of fear; it was the fear of death that God would kill me or send me to hell for everything I did wrong. I didn't know anything about the love of God and I'm sure I asked for forgiveness every night at bedtime. I think every Sunday I would go to the altar and "get saved again" confessing my sins out of fear and asking Jesus to come into my life when a teenager. There was a lack of teaching there for sure.

What is so weird and doesn't make any sense is that I also felt I was holier than anyone else because we were always judging and criticizing others because no one else met our standards. My parents were church hoppers because as soon as they didn't like something we left. If the pastor used notes he was not "led of the Spirit". If the pastor looked at the clock he was not "letting the Spirit move". If the lady at the organ or piano took off her shoes, for some reason that was wrong also, so we left. I was young and didn't understand I just knew they weren't holy like us.

When I was young my mother had a gospel tract titled "Others May! - You Cannot!" I think I read that when I was about 12 or 13 years old and it became my motto for life. I saw other kids who called themselves Christians doing things or saying things that I thought was a sin, so I determined to live my life the way a "real Christian" was supposed to be, which included all of our laws and rules of course. I still have the gospel tract.

In high school, about 1963, I started to date a girl at church. One Sunday morning she gave a message in tongues and someone gave the interpretation of the Spirit's message to the congregation also called "the body of Christ". These are two of the nine gifts of the Holy Spirit found in first Corinthians chapter 12 that I will touch on later. I thought I was sitting next to an angel. I immediately decided in my mind I wanted to marry this girl. She was so close to God, she had to be really holy to be used in the gifts of the Spirit.

After church I was taking her home and driving up the old Black Canyon Highway in Phoenix, with her sitting next to me. Oh was I in love and so excited! Then she made a comment and said, "Oh heck". I almost fell out of the car I was so shocked. I could not believe that this girl who gave a message in tongues could actually swear and say "heck". I took her straight home and never went out with her again. Why should I date her? I was much closer to God and holier than her because I didn't swear and say "heck" or "darn".

Later on I realized the enemy used that to keep me from pursuing anything about the baptism in the Holy Spirit because I was holier than any of my friends. I had become very prideful without knowing it and pride is the root of sin.

During the summer after high school graduation I worked for block layers building homes in Phoenix. I started working as an Iron worker the week before I turned 18 years old. My brothers were Journeyman Ironworkers and Certified Welders working on the Minuteman Missile sites in North Dakota and I went to find them. They took me to Fargo, ND to the office and I was given a Permit to work at the sites. They taught me how to use pliers and wire to tie reinforcement rods called "rebar" by using a broom handle across the back of a chair with vertical spindles. My right hand was so swollen every morning the first week that I had to exercise it on the way to the missile site so I could start tying rebar together again.

I continued to do ironwork during the summers in Michigan and Arizona. I was carrying rebar on my shoulder and tied them together before concrete was poured over them. When I would get to a new job site, the ironworkers would invite me to go and get a drink after work. One time I was asked to go and pick up a chick after work and "get some sex". My normal response was with a disgusted voice and an unkind look. I would say, "That is a sin, I'm a Christian and I don't do things like that". I may have had a sneer on my face and venom in my voice as I let them know how holy I was and what big sinners they were on their way to hell. That was how I let the "heathens" know I was a Christian.

In 1965, I was working on the Saginaw, Michigan Foundry and an Ironworker told me "you act like you are holier than thou". I was appalled and denied it but I didn't understand that he was actually speaking truth. I was blind to my own pride and

4

being like a "Pharisee", just like one of those in the Bible that Jesus called a "white washed wall". Who would ever want to be like me? However, no matter where I worked around the United States I read my Bible and tried to be a good Christian. I always found an Assembly of God church on Wednesday nights and on Sunday.

Of course I didn't say a word to "Christians" but I could see that they were not as holy as me. It was so engrained in me to be judgmental and critical in those early years of my life and I still struggle with that today. I thank the Holy Spirit for convicting me when I have those thoughts or make a comment about someone.

About 10 years ago I was walking and I saw a broken bottle on the sidewalk so I pushed the broken glass to the side. On the way back home I stopped to pick up the broken pieces so I squatted down and started with the big pieces, putting them into the base of the broken bottle. I looked to see if anyone was walking by to thank me. I kept picking up smaller pieces and hoped someone who had stopped at the traffic light next to me would roll down their window and tell me how awesome I was. Finally, I was picking up the tiniest pieces of broken glass waiting and watching for someone to praise me. I must have been there for at least 10 minutes and I finally stood up with those broken pieces of glass in my hand. When I stood up and looked around, there was still no one to thank me or praise me! I felt like throwing that broken bottle into the middle of the intersection.

The Holy Spirit spoke through a thought in my mind and said, "You still have pride!" I walked home with my head down carrying that broken bottle. What a humbling experience that day. Pride can be so subtle and start building up in our lives without our even realizing it at any age.

In 1975, I was working in Portland, Oregon as a federal agent and I found a Baptist church near the hotel. I'm sure I walked in with my guard up. When I got back to the hotel that

Sunday night from church I just kept worshipping the Lord because I had felt the presence of the Holy Spirit in that church. That was probably the first time I had attended a Baptist church. I had heard that Baptists didn't believe in the baptism in the Holy Spirit nor in speaking in tongues. So of course at that time in my life I didn't think they were as holy as me. That experience was so foreign to me when I saw how the Baptist loved the Lord and worshipped Him. What? God loves the Baptist too?

The Lord began opening my eyes as I saw God work in other denominations that were not "Pentecostal". When I was young I thought just Apostolic Lutherans were the only ones going to heaven. When I got older I assumed only the Pentecostals were going to heaven. I'm sure at one time I even thought the Carlson's were the only ones going to heaven. The Lord was starting to break down the walls of "prideful religion" that separated me from other believers. Boy did I have a lot to learn!

CHAPTER 2
THE PRICE OF UNFORGIVENESS

When I was 9 years old I was pulling weeds for neighbors in the hot summer Phoenix sun with no hat on and making 25 cents an hour and getting rich. About 1955, my two brothers and I all chipped in $5 and we bought a 110 pound set of weights. My big brother Jim was also physically big and compared to me he was huge. He was in the 8th grade and was up at 4:00am lifting weights. Then he delivered 100 newspapers before school. I tried lifting weights when it was convenient but I never got a muscular build like him. He probably weighed about 160 pounds when he first entered high school and I was 112 soaking wet my freshman year. I just wanted to be like my big brother.

Jim was good looking, muscular, was well liked and was not afraid to discuss the Bible with classmates of other religions. I would see him studying the Bible at home and I looked up to him in every way as he was my hero. I wanted to be just like Jim.

On the other hand, I was skinny, freckled face and I had fever blisters on my lips constantly from the sun in Phoenix. We didn't know about wearing a hat and my nose was red like a strawberry. In addition to my appearance, Jim always made fun of my lack of mental capacity. As a result, I had a gigantic inferiority complex and I used to brag in my high school years that I had the biggest inferiority complex west of the Mississippi River. That even sounds stupid now but I was the class clown and joked about everything, including myself.

The most painful thing that I recall is when I was 15 years old. Jim and I drove back to Michigan to see our cousins for the first time since I was 7. When we arrived on their street in Southfield, Michigan, Jim stopped the car and looked at me and said, "Jerry, the longer you keep your mouth shut the longer they won't know how stupid you are". I tried to keep my mouth shut and not say anything to my cousins, aunts and uncles, or anyone else unless they asked me a question. Jim didn't realize what he was doing, he was just a typical older brother who teased, made fun of and put me down not realizing the impact he was having in my life.

That verbal abuse went so deep that it took years for me to forgive Jim. If I shared that story with anyone I had venom in my voice from the pain. Praise the Lord I can share these things in a calm and soft voice and there is no pain, hurts or bitterness in me or in my voice. Oh yes, Jim asked for forgiveness and I will tell you about that later. My pain has made me an advocate for other little brothers and little sisters too.

If you are a big brother or big sister, do you need to ask the Lord to remind you of anything you did or said to your younger siblings that tore them down? That experience with Jim affected me until I was 50 years old when I retired from the U.S. Treasury Department. I never felt I was worth anything or any good at anything, which drove me to be very competitive, a perfectionist and people pleaser. By the way, I think that if someone made fun of their older brothers or sisters it could have had the same affects.

People just do not realize the power of their words. Proverbs 18:21 states that *Death and life are in the power of the tongue.* In high school I thought about suicide more than once but I knew that taking my life was not what God wanted. I kept trying to get the approval of man, like my supervisor and everyone else. I volunteered for extra work and helped others just to get approval. Words of praise and encouragement will bring life, but put downs and verbal abuse can bring death. Sometimes it is not easy to find something positive to say about a person but ask God to help you and watch the difference in their countenance when you say it.

The first time I remember having a positive thing said about me was after I graduated from high school. If anyone ever did compliment me, I wasn't aware of it. My brother Jim was all I cared about. I wanted his approval and love. I'm sorry to say that I teased him just to get his attention. One time he couldn't find his pocket knife so I acted as though I'd hid it, even though I didn't know where it was. He chased me out of the house and I don't remember what happened after that. No, he didn't knock me out or kill me, but maybe close to it.

When I was 17 years old after graduating from high school in 1963, a friend and I were seeing how much weight we could lift. We brought our weights together after church in the 115 degree heat of the Phoenix summer sun. I weighed 132 pounds and lifted 190 pounds over my head. I tried lifting 195 pounds and could not lock my right elbow. I was devastated to say the least because I wanted to lift more than Jim. He was the fullback on the football team and weighed 210 pounds when he graduated. He had lifted 200 pounds over his head and I wanted to beat Jim. I have never been a numbers guy and you already guessed it. I've been a criminal investigator, not an auditor or CPA.

A few weeks later another friend of mine and I met after church on Sunday and we were wrestling in the back yard. His dad was a general contractor and was building a church in Phoenix. My brother Jim worked on that church with my friend. When my friend finally pinned me to the ground he got up and said, "Wow, you are strong! You are the strongest guy I have ever wrestled. The only reason I finally pinned you is because you don't know the wrestling techniques like me being on the wrestling team. If you would have gone out for wrestling you could have taken the state championship you are so strong. Yeah, Jim said you were strong!"

What? Jim said I was strong? The first positive thing said about me after 17 years came from someone else but Jim had said it. That was amazing to me and that one word of praise lifted my self-worth, which I had never experienced before.

It must have been 20 years later when I realized I was actually stronger than Jim. He weighed 210 and lifted 200 pounds. I lifted my weight of 132 pounds, plus almost half my weight of 60 more pounds totaling 190. Jim should have lifted his weight plus half of his weight totaling 315 pounds. I could not believe it. And all those many years he called me weenie arm, pencil neck and made other demeaning remarks. I opened my shirt one time before I had hair on my chest and I told Jim, "hair doesn't grow on steel" and he said, "hair doesn't grow on sawdust either". That was a truthful statement! Back then I could never win but it's funny now.

The power of unforgiveness started to open my eyes and penetrate my heart when I was in Vietnam in 1967 and 1968. The Lord started to help me in in the area of forgiveness as I thought about my brother Jim, and then say, "I forgive you brother". I had to keep peeling off the unforgiveness every time I was reminded of a comment or hurt. It is like peeling the layers off of an onion which I've heard others say.

Some years later after I got back from Vietnam Jim and I had a long talk and he was so sorry he treated me like that growing up and he asked me for forgiveness. We forgave each other and our forgiveness was a sweet time. In fact, Jim started sending me a birthday card to tell me how proud he was of me and what a special little brother I was. In fact, he wrote a special birthday card for my birthday in October 2018, just before he died unexpectedly. It still brings tears to my eyes thinking of it, and I still have the birthday card. I miss him so much!

Through the remaining years of our lives, Jim and I became so close, sharing what God was revealing to us in the Bible and what the Lord was doing in and through our lives. I shared with Jim that the Lord had used our experience to give me a tender heart for younger siblings and to teach on the power of our words. We have wept together and our love for each other grew deeper.

My dad was 41 when I was born. To me he was an "old man" and when I was 10 he was already 51, and acted like an old man. He had a rough life. He was raised on a farm and worked on it, since age didn't make a difference back in those days. He was in 6th grade 3 years until they kicked him out of school. He said the reason they kicked him out is because he was shaving. Dad always had a sense of humor and laughed and teased all the time. I picked up the teasing part from my dad. At 14 years of age dad went to work in the copper mine in Northern Michigan, and also went to work on the commercial fishing boats on Lake Superior, so he had a hard life.

Dad never took me fishing or camping or anything fathers usually do with their sons. Well should I say, "Anyone can be a father but it takes someone special to be a dad". If he wanted to go rock hunting we got to go along. He was like a grandfather because he seemed so old to me but he didn't treat me like a grandson. Don't forget now, there were no books, seminars or conferences on how to be a Godly father or Godly husband back in those days. Also kids were to be seen and not heard. You never answered back and we'd get a good "whip'n"! When I was a senior in high school everything changed when I got more than a "whip'n".

It was in an English class where kids were throwing spit wads. The teacher threatened 4 or 5 of them and said she would send them to the principal's office if they didn't stop. She finally named 2 kids and said, "Does anyone else want to go to the principal's office?" I had not thrown any spit wads but I jokingly lifted my hand and said, "I would go, but I need to go to the library". She said, "Well you can go to the principal's office anyway". So off I went to the principal's office. It doesn't always pay to be the class clown!

Needless to say the principle wrote a letter to my parents. A few days later my dad was waiting for me at the front door. He was never home from work this early. I opened the screen door as he opened the front door. He handed me the letter to read. As I stood there and read the letter I'm sure I started to smile, at least on the inside. However, I'm sure I didn't laugh but I could have. I knew I was NOT GUILTY of throwing spit wads I was just the class clown as usual. When I looked up,

11

dad was not smiling and he had fire in his eyes. He told me to get in the bedroom and take my pants down. He never asked me why I threw spit wads in class or anything else.

I should have been a disobedient child and run away from home while I had the chance. But I was obedient and went in like a dumb sheep to the slaughter. Remember, dad was angry! Well, he used his 2" wide leather belt and you get the idea. I told the coach what happened and he was kind enough to let me stay in street clothes until I healed. I was not able to dress out for Physical Education (PE) for many weeks. My grade went down from an A to a C for that 6 week period. I was hurting to say the least under those clothes but it only hurt when I was walking, standing, sitting or lying in bed.

I hated my father after that and never spoke to him unless he questioned me. When I graduated from high school I left home. I knew I could survive on my own because I had been working in grocery stores since I was 14 years old. In my Junior and Senior year I worked about 35 hours a week in the produce section. I sure didn't need anyone to take care of me so I left home and knew I could take care of myself.

By the way, I told you earlier that we moved a lot. I was at the same school in 4th, 5th and 6th grades and at the same high school the last two years. The remaining 7 school years I changed schools 17 times. It is a miracle that I'm normal, although most of my friends question that.

When I was living at home, my dad required that I pay $15 a week for room and board. I also had to pay for my car insurance; gas and spending money out of my $30 a week take home pay. Just three years later I went into the military.

In January 1967, I went into the U.S. Army and in March I was selected for the Military Police Academy. After the Academy Barb and I got married. In July I went to K-9 training to be a dog handler at Lackland Air Force Base. While in training, a dog team (a dog and his handler) would be scouting in the brush for the enemy in an attack suit while the other guys were sitting around smoking and visiting. I took my dog "Boots" to the side and I worked with him in all the commands. I taught him other things like crawling. I figured we would be doing a lot of crawling in Vietnam.

On a Friday night before graduation Boots and I were selected to replace two other dog teams that had been training for 8 weeks to put on demonstrations at our graduation. Boots and I demonstrated long leash obedience with a 30 foot leash at graduation and some other things that I forget now. That competitive attitude resulted in my receiving an Honor Graduate Award from Lackland AFB.

Boots and I left for Vietnam the first of December 1967, after I took Barbara back to Phoenix from Fort Carson and set up a trailer house near the hospital where she was hired to work as a nurse. She had graduated from Nursing College in May 1967, and that is when we got married.

The first night of patrol in Vietnam I saw the biggest Javelina I had ever seen. I was from Arizona and I knew that Javelina, also called Peccari, were mean and vicious wild pigs. They had huge tusks even though they only weighed 20 to 30 pounds. Boots and I were dropped off at midnight to start patrol at Cam Ranh Bay. I threw my M16 over my shoulder and stood there for 20 minutes to let my eyes get adjusted to the dark. I then told Boots, "Okay boy let's go".

We had only taken two steps when out of a tunnel in the brush came the biggest Javelina I had even seen. This one appeared to weigh about 350 pounds with a head bigger than a basketball. It came walking towards us within 4 to 6 feet of Boots and went into a tunnel at my right side at the 4:00 O'clock position. It was as though we were invisible. Boots and I froze. I had no time to get my M16 off my shoulder. I think Boots and I both stopped breathing. I took the rifle off my shoulder and held the handle with my finger on the trigger for the rest of the night.

In the morning I told my buddies about the big giant Javelina. They said, "Carlson that wasn't a Javelina that was a wild boar". I was not from California then and I knew nothing about wild boars. I do now and they are big and vicious and will attack you. I realized later that the Lord blinded that wild boar as it walked right toward us. It should've attacked both of us and ripped us both to shreds. That was just the start of God's protecting hand over both of us in our introduction to Vietnam.

One other experience of God's guidance happened in Cam Ranh Bay during the 2 week period before we were sent to our duty stations to start night patrol. One Sunday night before we went on patrol the Sergeant said, "Okay, we are going to start shipping you out tomorrow so let me know in the morning where you want to go". What? Where do I want to volunteer to die? The men started talking about various bases where they wanted to go but I knew nothing of where the bases were located in Vietnam.

I went on patrol at midnight and started praying. I walked and prayed until 4:00 AM at which time I had a peace come over me. I had no idea where to volunteer to go but I had this amazing peace in my mind and heart. In the morning when I came off patrol I told the Sergeant to send me wherever they needed me. I was sent to Camp Radcliff near An Khe in the Central Highlands.

I received a letter from Barbara in late January. She asked if I was okay. She said she was in church on that same Sunday morning and felt prompted to start praying for me during the service. After the service she went to the altar and continued to pray for me until 1:00 O'clock. At that time she had a real peace come over her and she went home. I wrote to her and told her what happened on that Sunday night.

She got my letter about the end of March. Isn't God amazing? I had a peace come over me at 4:00 AM Monday morning and she had a peace at 1:00 PM on Sunday in Arizona, the exact same time in Vietnam. There is no distance in prayer!

While in Vietnam the Lord started doing a deep work in me to forgive my dad also. I knew there was a good chance I could die in Vietnam. I believed that if I didn't forgive my dad and my brother that the Lord would not forgive me. That was a sobering thought because Jesus and the Bible gave us clear directions about forgiving, Matthew 6:14-15.

The Lord started to convict me of my unforgiveness toward Jim and the hatred I had for my dad. As I struggled with forgiving them the pain went deep. I had to start asking the Lord to help me to forgive them and I had to ask over and over each time memories came to me. The Lord started that healing process and I think it was easier to forgive my dad because it was a one-time event. I think it took longer for me to forgive Jim because it was over a 17 year period of my life growing up.

On November 1, 1968, President Johnson started the bombing halt of North Vietnam so we were under major attack. Only America will tell the enemy our plans so they have time to prepare their attack on us. Some of my buddies were afraid to go out on night patrol since they were "short" meaning they were close to being sent home. They paid me $10 to pull their night patrol, so I worked my patrol and their patrol every night for about 3 months. I never thought I would come out alive so I thought I might as well patrol all night to stay alert and pray. We were under major attack since November 1. Things were blowing up and burning around us as rockets and mortars came in and still burning the day I left Camp Radcliff.

Around December 4 or 5 we got in a jeep and I am sure Boots was excited as we headed to the landing zone that day. I expected that we would get blown out of the sky by the Vietcong, but as that military plane got higher and higher I started breathing again. We headed to Cam Rahn Bay to start processing out of Vietnam and I finally made it home to my bride of 19 months.

Hugging my dad for the first time in December 1968, after almost 6 years was a strange feeling. At first it was like hugging an oak tree but he finally started to hug me back. Dad had never hugged me or told me that he loved me growing up. That was a normal thing for most dads in those days and I didn't know any different. We were born to help and work around the home and farm. I started telling dad that I loved him but he never said those words to me.

After finishing 20 units in May 1969, I graduated from Phoenix Junior College and we moved to Flagstaff where I was hired as a Deputy Sheriff. I started to attend Northern Arizona University to obtain my Bachelor of Science degree in Police Science and Administration with minors in Psychology and Sociology. I never really knew what career to pursue so I started in engineering since my two brothers started that way but never graduated. The Lord gave me direction for my life by selecting me for the Military Police. Thank you Lord!

Now for one quick story as a Deputy. The Sheriff allowed one of the prisoners to go home on Saturdays since he was "a good boy". I was working the jail when he came back that evening and he emptied his pockets on the counter. I searched him and didn't find anything. Then I looked through the things he laid on the counter. I observed what appeared to be an almost new pack of cigarettes because the pack had just been torn open enough to remove a couple of cigarettes. I tilted the pack on an angle so I could see inside the package more clearly and only saw cigarettes. Then I tore the top off all the way back and there in the back of the pack were about 6 marijuana cigarettes. Off to prison he went for smuggling drugs into a jail facility. The jail was a federal holding facility since we were on the main Highway 66 and we arrested escaped felons and others with federal warrants.

My parents had moved to Camp Verde before we moved to Flagstaff. It was 55 miles away so Barbara and I enjoyed going to visit them. I was glad to cut firewood and do things to help my dad and mom. They would come to Flagstaff to get groceries and stopped to visit us over that two year period where our two sons were born. I had a chance to love my dad and show him my love because all the pain was gone.

On September 20, 1971, I was hired by the U.S. Treasury Department as a Criminal Investigator. I have to laugh when I think about my background security clearance. When we hire a new agent it is a top priority and anywhere they lived, worked and went to school, leads are sent out all over the United States for other agents to do the investigation. We can normally complete the security clearance in two weeks. It took them from June to September to do my clearance since I worked all over the United States, working and staying in motels for 3 days or 2 weeks working construction, iron work and other jobs.

I was assigned to help open the new office in Fresno, California in November 1971, after finishing the Treasury Law Enforcement Officers Training School (TLEOTS) in Washington, D.C. We only got to see the folks a couple times a year after that. Then the Lord took dad home unexpectedly in April of 1975, at 69 years of age.

We flew from California and went to see dad in the Cottonwood hospital. He was not able to respond in ICU so I never got to say goodbye to him, but the Lord helped me to forgive dad in that year in Vietnam. I never confronted my dad and he never asked me for forgiveness so we never talked about it. But the most important thing was that I had forgiven him and my life reflected that forgiveness when I got home from Vietnam. What a big difference forgiveness makes in our relationships and in our own lives.

Sometimes when a person hurts us it is better to share with them as soon as possible the pain they have caused otherwise it starts turning to bitterness and we live with that pain. This can be done in a kind, tender voice asking if they realized what they said or did. They may not have realized what they did or said and it gives them an opportunity to explain without putting them on the defense. If you decide to share your pain years later with a person you love, it might hurt them deeply. They probably didn't realize how they hurt you and it might not be worth putting them through that kind of pain. If that is your case, I encourage you to forgive them, open your hand and release that past hurt to the Lord.

Oh my friend, unforgiveness has a price to pay! I was the one who was tormented and in pain every time I thought about what happened to me. Those that hurt you don't even realize it most of the time and may not have intended to hurt you. Oh yes, there are those who purposely do things to hurt others, I know! Talk to the Lord about it, He understands.

It's amazing, after 17 years of verbal abuse I started working as a Criminal Investigator with the U.S. Treasury Department. I opened the new office in Fresno with another agent and a supervisor on November 15, 1971. My new partner and I would go on a break and he would light up a cigarette and purposely blow smoke in my face. Yes I wanted to take him for a walk and beat the tar out of him but I just held my breath. I would need him for a backup if we were making an arrest but he enjoyed doing things to aggravate me so I just forgave him on the inside and didn't say or do anything.

Three more agents came in and we were all new so headquarters sent a senior agent to our office. He verbally abused me for 7 years. He tried to break me down from living my life as a Christian. With his superiority complex, he also felt the need to harass and agitate some of my fellow co-workers. Several agents transferred to other offices because of the way they were treated. One of my good friends gave up his career as a Federal Agent.

During those years I asked that senior agent to come into the conference room. I asked him "What have I done to you that makes you treat me with such disrespect?" He never really answered me, so I asked him to forgive me anyway for whatever I had done. In 1975, after 3 years of taking his abuse I walked into his office and I was angry and fed up with how he treated me.

He was about six foot six and sitting down at his desk so we were almost eye level when I walked into his office. I pointed at him and said, "I'm sick and tired of you" and that is all I got to say. I didn't even get to finish giving him a piece of my mind when he looked up at me as I was starting to speak and he got the biggest smile on his face. He pointed at me with one hand and started slapping the desk with the other hand and said, "I got you, I got you, I finally got you!" Even as he said that I immediately said, "I'm sorry I should not have gotten angry at you, please forgive me". I had a lot of forgiving to do for what he put me through for another 4 years. He left our agency after 7 years but you have not heard the rest of the story of what the Lord did.

It was about February of 1979, and I was the first one in the office early in the morning. As I walked in the door I just felt prompted to go over to the secretary's desk where the calendar was hanging. I lifted up the calendar to May and I circled the "15th" and I knew that the senior agent would be gone on that day. A coworker came into the office later and I took him over to show him the calendar. I lifted it up to May and showed him where I had circled the "15th". I told him that the agent would be gone on that day and he asked me how I knew and I said, "I just know".

On the 15th of May, that agent was at his desk whispering all day. Two weeks later he was gone. We found out he had been asked to leave the agency on May 15. I believe that was a gift of the Holy Spirit working in my life that day and I believe it was a word of knowledge according to 1 Corinthians 12:8. I would have never known that by my own intellect. I had forgiven him many times and finally the Lord removed him from my life. I thought my testing was over!

Between 1985 and 1990 I had a new supervisor that tried to get rid of me because I was a Christian. He was doing everything he could to try and make my life miserable. He would make negative comments about me in front of other agents. He would return my reports over and over for rewriting, which rarely happened in the previous 14 years. I just kept forgiving him and being submissive to his leadership.

One day he was looking at an application outside his office door and stated loud enough for everyone to hear, "I'm not hiring this guy, we don't need any more Christians around here". Apparently the applicant had reported something on his application about attending Bible School or something related to Christianity. If I had not been productive or if I had been a problem agent he could have fired me, however, I had the most prosecutions during 3 years of his leadership. I had worked major fraud cases at the Ogden Internal Revenue Service (IRS) Center, the Fresno IRS Service Center and in San Francisco I investigated the Bureau of the Mint, the Bureau of Engraving and The Comptroller of the Currency.

Before my supervisor was promoted to Deputy Chief in 1990, I remember a friend at church telling me this story. My supervisor had gone to a local construction store where my friend worked. My friend saw my supervisor's Treasury Department badge and he said, "Oh I have a friend who works for the Treasury Department, Jerry Carlson". The supervisor said, "Yes, Jerry works for me" and then he proceeded to tell my friend, "Jerry walks what he talks". Wow, my supervisor said that? After all he was putting me through?

My supervisor was promoted in 1990 and moved to Walnut Creek, California. I retired in January 1996. In March of 1997, I called that former supervisor because he had a home in Fresno and came home on the weekends from the Bay Area. I invited him to a Men's breakfast at my church. He accepted. We were signing up for Promise Keepers in Fresno and I asked him if he would like to go with me and he said yes.

After Promise Keepers I asked him if he would like to do a Bible study with me and he said yes. I led him and 6 more guys through the Experiencing God Bible study by Henry Blackaby, at his home! We became brothers in Christ and shared the Word together, having lunch together often until he passed away with cancer from Agent Orange a few years ago. We had both served in Vietnam in 1967-68, but didn't know each other there. We were both exposed to Agent Orange since 1968 was the heaviest spraying of that chemical.

During those 25 years as a federal agent I had a lot of forgiving to do at work. Isn't it interesting, how words have so much power? We can destroy someone with our words and it may affect them for decades and even a life time if God doesn't get invited in to help. As I mentioned Proverbs 18:21 earlier, I actually quoted it like this, "Life and death are in the power of the tongue". A few years ago the Holy Spirit checked me and I felt I had to look at it again. I realized it actually says *Death and life are in the power of the tongue*. Wow, death can come first until the tongue is changed, which really speaks from the heart. If you have said things to people or abused them in any way, ask them to forgive you. They may accept or reject your apology and that's okay because that will be their choice.

There is a big difference in saying "I'm sorry" and saying "Would you please forgive me?" When we ask for forgiveness, then that puts the responsibility on their shoulders to accept our asking for forgiveness and to forgive us. That has now been taken off of our shoulders and we are set free.

For years, no, I'm sorry to say it was decades, I would tell Barbara I was sorry when I said something or did something that hurt her. In 2005, the Lord used Luke in my life again. I discovered I was an expert in "self-defense". I blamed traffic, people or anything else I could use to cast blame. It has been a process of learning to accept responsibility and saying, "Angel, I was wrong, Christ would never have talked to you in that tone of voice, would you please forgive me?"

Dear friend, pray and ask the Lord to give you a teachable spirit and the Lord will be glad to reveal things in your life to make you more like Him. It's never too late to learn! Just be ready for someone close to you to speak truth into your life. Remember that truth is hard to swallow but once it is inside it turns sweet. Don't react, just listen and then pray for God to show you how to work that "out of your life".

At the end of April, 2018, I went back to North Carolina to see my brother Ralph. He had just been released from the hospital for the second time and I was not sure he would live. The first of May, Jim drove up from Bear Creek, NC to be with us and we visited for almost two hours in the rehab center. We had a chance to tell stories and laugh together. Then we made sure there was nothing that needed forgiveness. All was well between us 3 brothers so each of us took turns praying for the other brothers and we hugged each other and wept. Ralph passed away on July 12 and Jim unexpectedly passed away less than 3 months later on October 11. I can't emphasize it enough, what peace forgiveness brings.

Other people, like my co-workers or supervisor, can make comments, tease or do things that causes deep pain in us that they are not even aware of. It is because we have something we are carrying from our past that triggers that hurt. When that other person makes a comment it can be like peeling the scab off of an old injury. It bleeds so easily again until Jesus heals the deep wound.

Remember that God is love and "LOVE ALWAYS INITIATES" taking the first step. Jesus took the first step in loving us, dying for us and drawing us to the Father. Sometimes we need to take the first step by going to that person and asking for forgiveness if we even think that we have hurt them. I have done that and sometimes they never even felt that I had done or said anything offensive. However, at least my conscience is clear now. Maybe it is dying to my pride and humbling myself to go to them to ask for forgiveness.

One of the classes I used to teach at Central Valley Teen Challenge was titled "The Price of Unforgiveness". I spent two class periods on that one topic. I also assigned homework on it because it is such a critical part of our Christian walk as I have learned firsthand.

As we look at Ephesians 4:17-19 it talks about our former life of walking in the flesh. The chapter goes on to explain what our life in Christ should look like. When you come to the end of Chapter 4, verse 32 it says *And be kind to one another, tenderhearted, forgiving one another, even as God in Christ forgave you.* Forgiving others even as God in Christ has forgiven me. Wow, that sounds important.

When we read Matthew 6:14-15, Jesus is speaking and said, *For if you forgive men their trespasses, your heavenly Father will also forgive you. But if you do not forgive men their trespasses, neither will your Father forgive your trespasses.* Now it sounds a little more serious right?

In Matthew 18:21-35, Jesus is telling the story of the unforgiving servant. He had been forgiven his large debt by the master but turned around and refused to forgive the small debt a fellow servant owed him. In verses 34 and 35, Jesus said, *And his master was angry, and delivered him to the torturers until he should pay all that was due to him. So My heavenly Father will also do to you if each of you, from his heart, doesn't forgive his brother his trespasses.* Now that sounds like we are in real trouble if we don't forgive others!

We are the ones who are tortured with pain every time we think of that person or situation. It is like drinking poison and hoping it affects that person. The word torture is used in many versions of the Bible so it was not a mistake!

Could it be that when we hold bitterness and unforgiveness that we end up being tortured and that thing will eat at us day and night? I know that from experience! It affects our relationship, our thinking, sometimes our words and may even affect our actions. Can the Holy Spirit work freely and fully when the vessel is not clean inside? I believe that the unforgiveness we hold onto can hinder the flow of the Holy Spirit in and through our lives. Did you notice I said "in our lives" and "through our lives"? Yes He can still use us in spite of our faults and weaknesses but how much more effective could the Holy Spirit be in our lives if we stop carrying that baggage of unforgiveness with us?

A powerful example of forgiveness is in Acts 7:60, when Stephen was being stoned to death, he asked God not to charge them with that sin. What about Luke 23:34, when Jesus was dying on the cross and He said, *Father forgive them, for they do not know what they do.* Dear friend, ask the Lord to help you forgive anyone who may have hurt you in some way. Just keep asking the Lord to help you forgive them every time that thought or feeling comes back in your mind.

By the way, have you ever stolen something or lied to someone? Maybe it was before you became a Christian or you were a new Christian. Here is an opportunity to set things right. Ask that person for forgiveness and offer to make restitution for what you stole or the damage you caused. Hopefully the person will see that Jesus is making a difference in your life. This is an opportunity to bring glory to Jesus. He has changed you and you can be a witness to that person. Pray and ask God for direction and His timing to see that person or maybe send them a letter. It is always best to see them eye to eye if at all possible.

Another thing that has helped me forgive others is when I started to realize how much I needed forgiveness. I wanted to know more of what Jesus went through on the cross. I went on a 40 day "Daniel Fast" leading up to Easter. Like Daniel in the Bible, Daniel 19:3, I ate nothing pleasant or that I liked. My heart was focused on how much Jesus suffered in order to forgive my sins. That Easter season was very special and I have been able to forgive others because of Jesus love, mercy and His grace for me. You will find that life is much better if you have more mercy for others and you won't get offended so easily.

You may need to share your pains and hurts with someone and I highly recommend finding a good solid Christian ministry that will walk you through it. The Pregnancy Care Center is a life affirming ministry and helps women who are considering abortion. They help them see the value of life so they can make an informed decision.

Thank the Lord for the prison ministries and other ministries that are pointing people to Jesus and Him crucified. When people experience the love and forgiveness that God has for them, it even helps prisoners to forgive others. I also think of the ministries at various churches that touch so many areas of our lives like Celebrate Recovery for example.

We all know someone or know a family who has a loved one addicted to drugs or alcohol. I think of the 1400 Teen Challenge Ministry campuses around the world in 129 countries that brings hope to addicts through a relationship with Jesus Christ. Addicts find freedom through this ministry. Changed lives leave this one year residential discipleship program.

Relationships with families and even with some spouses are restored. The majority are adult campuses where men and women become an asset to society and find jobs. The teen campuses help them learn to become responsible adults. The courts are sending men and women, including teens to Teen Challenge because of the great success rate. Jesus Christ is the one who changes lives and brings hope.

If you have been addicted to anything or lived a life of crime and ruined people's lives or anything else, I want to give you a word of caution. You must use wisdom when you share your testimony of how God forgave you and delivered you out of that. I have heard some former drug addicts share how God had them go through their drug addictions so they can go and witness to other drug addicts.

That is absolutely the farthest thing from the truth. God would never send you into an addiction or allow you to experience addictions in your life so He can use you to help others! He sent Jesus to set us free from sin and addictions. Your addictions, life of crime or life of rebellion was your choice, so don't give God the credit for it. As a result of your choices and your addictions, whatever takes top priority in your life, when you submit to God He can deliver you. It is all a matter of our free will and choices where we end up, either walking with Jesus or in sin.

Going through the verbal abuse and the trials with all the hurts and pain sure doesn't make sense at the time if you are in the midst of it now. As I look back I can see how God used those experiences in my life to help me learn to forgive others and not fight for my rights. If I die to myself so Christ can be alive in me then a dead man has no rights.

As you are reading now do you see how the Lord has used my experiences to share and also teach on the power of our words as well as the price of unforgiveness? God knew my brother Jim before I did and He knew my coworkers and what they would do to me. I think that God can allow us to go through experiences that are not meant for us personally but that He can use our trials and suffering for His glory.

As a result of being verbally abused for 17 years and even though I was only "whipped" once, I had hatred and unforgiveness as a result of those experiences, which was my choice. However, in Vietnam the Holy Spirit worked in my life to start learning to forgive and start loving. Agape love (God's love) started working in me and I realize now writing this book that was the preparation and training for me to learn to forgive my coworker and boss. Had it not been for Jim and my

26

dad in my life I could have been very mean and not acted Christ-like in my office.

Learning to forgive and have patience I also learned to turn the other cheek as it reads in Matthew 5:38-39 *You have heard that is was said, 'An eye for an eye and a tooth for a tooth.' But I tell you not to resist an evil person. But whoever slaps you on your right cheek, turn the other to him also.*

Please don't think I have it all together, I am still growing. In addition, this book would never have been written had it not been for my life experiences growing up. I rejoice in my Lord and praise Him for what He has done and is still doing in my life at my age.

As I have said, the most important thing in life is to repent, accept God's forgiveness by faith and surrender our lives to Christ. I was going to say that finding a godly spouse is the second most important thing in life, but when I stop to think about it, I believe walking in forgiveness is the second most important thing on this earth. Then, find a godly spouse!

Unforgiveness will affect your marriage, family and others. It can even affect your health. One of my Vietnam buddies told me recently that he also dealt with unforgiveness and I quote Rich, "It is too high of a price to pay!"

CHAPTER 3
WHO IS THIS HOLY SPIRIT?

What an inspiration by the authors who have written books on the Holy Spirit and the Baptism in the Holy Spirit. I also love to read about men and women of God and how the Holy Spirit has used them because it inspires and challenges me. Please take advantage of some of my sources in the Recommended Reading section.

Some of what I'm going to share now in this chapter about the Holy Spirit is from notes in the back of The New Spirit Filled Life Bible. I want to acknowledge Dr. Jack Hayford the Editor who is an excellent Bible teacher. I've had the privilege of being under his teaching. This Bible has so much information regarding the Holy Spirit, the baptism in the Holy Spirit as well as the gifts of the Spirit. The latest "Third Edition" update is titled The Spirit Filled Life Bible.

When I read in the Old Testament I see where the Holy Spirit was there at creation in Genesis 1:2 ...*And the Spirit of God was hovering over the face of the waters.* As God spoke the Word (Jesus is the Word, John 1:1-4) He created everything into existence by speaking it except man, because He formed man from the dust of the ground. So the Holy Spirit is part of the Trinity. I cannot fathom or understand the Trinity, I don't need to. The Bible shows it and that settles it!

In Zechariah 12:1, it reads, *Thus says the LORD, who stretches out the heavens, lays the foundation of the earth, and forms the spirit of man within him.* So everyone has a spirit within them. God wants us to walk with Him in fellowship and our spirit needs to be born again.

We have been created in the image of God who is a Trinity consisting of God the Father, God the Son and God the Holy Spirit. We have a body, soul and spirit. Our soul is made up of three parts, our mind or intellect, our will and our emotions.

Look what the Bible says about the Holy Spirit having a mind, will and emotions.

In Romans 8:27 it reads *Now He who searches the hearts knows what the **mind** of the Spirit is, because He makes intercession for the saints according to the will of God (emphasis added).*

In 1 Corinthians 12:11, we see the Spirit has a will, *But one and the same Spirit works all these things, distributing to each one individually as He **wills** (emphasis added).*

And in Ephesians 4:30 it shows that the Spirit has emotions, *And do not **grieve** the Holy Spirit of God, by whom you were sealed for the day of redemption (emphasis added).*

The Holy Spirit possesses the divine characteristics of the Triune Godhead, that of the Father and the Son. The Holy Spirit is eternal (existing forever without beginning or ending), He is omnipresent (present everywhere at the same time), He is omnipotent (having all and unlimited power) and He is omniscient (all knowing). The word "omni" is a Latin prefix meaning "all" or "every".

In Hebrews 9:14, He is eternal. Reading in Psalm 139:7-10 it reflects He is Omnipresent. He is Omnipotent in Luke 1:35 and He is also Omniscient as we read in 1 Corinthians 2:10-11.

When we read the scriptures in the Old Testament and New Testament we have seen that the Holy Spirit has been at work from the beginning of time. Here are some attributes of the Holy Spirit.

The Holy Spirit:

2 Peter 1:21	Reveals
John 14:26	Teaches
Hebrews 10:15	Witnesses
Romans 8:26	Intercedes
Revelation 2:7	Speaks
Acts 16:6-7	Commands

John 15:26	Testifies
John 14:15-17	He has a relationship with us
Ephesians 4:30	He can be grieved
Acts 5:3	He can be lied to
Matthew 12:31-32	He can be blasphemed

The Holy Spirit is called by many names, for example when you read the Bible you will find some of these titles for the Holy Spirit.

The Spirit of God	Genesis 1:2
The Spirit of Christ	Romans 8:9
The Comforter	John 14:16
The Holy Spirit	Acts 19:6
The Holy Spirit of promise	Ephesians 1:13
The Spirit of Truth	John 14:17
The Spirit of grace	Zechariah 12:10
The Spirit of life	1Peter 3:18
The Spirit of adoption	Romans 8:15
The Spirit of holiness	Ephesians 4:30
The Eternal Spirit	Hebrews 9:14

The Holy Spirit is illustrated with symbols such as:

Fire and wind	Acts 2:1,2
Water	John 7:37-39
A Seal	Ephesians 1:13
Oil	Acts 10:38
Like (or as) a dove	John 1:32, Matthew 3:16

So many times we see the Holy Spirit pictured as a white dove but the Spirit of God descended "like" or "as" a dove on Jesus in Matthew 3:16. However, it was not a dove but have you noticed the gentleness of a dove? Doves are not aggressive like a hawk and doves do not fight like geese for examples. I see them land softly and they sure don't squawk and scream like some birds. I hear doves cooing in that low soft sound. I can imagine the resemblance to the gentleness of the Holy Spirit descending on Jesus when He was baptized in water.

The Holy Spirit is a person and yet he is present everywhere in the Spirit realm. He is at work in those lives who have submitted to Christ. A person can be born again of the Spirit and have eternal life but never desire to grow in their relationship with Jesus. They are content to go to church but may not spend time reading the Bible or praying. The Holy Spirit wants to do more in our lives but if a person is not hungry for more of Him, then I truly believe that He is limited in what He can do in that life.

Some people have a desire to "walk in the Spirit". Basically, "walking in the Spirit" means that a person has submitted their life to God and they want Jesus Christ to be Lord of their life in every area. They also desire to be sensitive to and obedient to the inner voice of the Holy Spirit who can speak to them by bringing thoughts to their mind for example. I will explain and give examples of how the Holy Spirit speaks to us in a later chapter.

The Holy Spirit can speak to us because He wrote the Bible, in 2 Peter 1:21, *For prophecy never came by the will of man, but holy men of God spoke as they were moved by the Holy Spirit.* A person can learn to just sit quietly and listen to what thoughts come to them as they spend time in prayer.

In Galatians 5:16-26 we see the difference between walking in the Spirit and walking in our own carnal ways called "the flesh", which we refer to as "the old man". That is before Christ does the work of renewing us into the "new man" by the Holy Spirit when we accept His forgiveness and choose to live for Christ. I will expound on that in the next chapter.

In John 16:7 Jesus said; *Nevertheless, I tell you the truth. It is to your advantage that I go away; for if I do not go away, the Helper will not come to you; but if I depart, I will send Him to you.* In the Amplified Bible the word "Helper" is identified as Comforter, Advocate, Intercessor-Counselor, Strengthener, and Standby.

32

CHAPTER 4
TAKING THE FIRST STEP

A person cannot be baptized in the Holy Spirit unless they have the Holy Spirit living in them as a result of salvation. I will be showing you a demonstration later that may help you see the difference in being filled (indwelt) with the Spirit at the time of salvation and being baptized in the Holy Spirit, which can happen at the time of salvation or later.

In my time alone with the Lord this morning and in His Word, I read in John 3:3, where Jesus told Nicodemus, *Most assuredly, I say to you, unless one is born again, he cannot see the kingdom of God.* In verse 5 Jesus said, *Most assuredly, I say to you, unless one is born of water and the Spirit, he cannot enter the kingdom of God.*

When Jesus said born of water I believe he is talking about natural child birth. In verse 6, Jesus said, *That which is born of the flesh is flesh and that which is born of the Spirit is spirit.* I also know that being baptized in water is a command of Jesus Christ. In Matthew 28:18-20 Jesus said, *All authority has been given to me in heaven and on earth. Go therefore and make disciples of all nations, baptizing them in the name of the Father and of the Son and of the Holy Spirit. Teaching them to observe all things that I have commanded you; and lo, I am with you always, even to the end of the age.*

Some theologians see verse 5 *born of water and the Spirit* as water baptism being the act of salvation in a person's life when they are born of the Spirit. Admitting they are a sinner and need Jesus in their life they get baptized in water immediately. Going down under the water signifying they are dying to the "old man" or "flesh" even as Jesus died and went into the grave. Then as the person comes up out of the water it symbolizes that they are raised to new life in Jesus, just as Jesus was resurrected to new life that morning He walked out of the tomb on resurrection day.

In Luke 3:3 it reads that John came preaching a baptism of repentance for the remission of sins. In Acts 19:4-5, Paul was in Ephesus and said, *John indeed baptized with a baptism of repentance...When they heard this they were baptized in the name of the Lord Jesus.* John the Baptist had been a voice crying in the wilderness to prepare the way of Christ coming and that people should repent and be baptized for salvation.

Now other theologians see water baptism as another step of obedience to Jesus command and it can take place at a later time, hopefully not long after. Either way, when we come to Christ a whole new world opens to us, the spirit world. Being baptized in water is like stepping through another door in our walk and relationship with Christ. It is often called "An outward testimony of an inward work". If a person gets baptized in water at a later time it is another confession of their faith in God that helps them to walk out their life in a Christ like manner, giving them more boldness.

As a result of these differing views, some churches baptize in water as part of the process or act of salvation immediately and other churches baptize after a person's confession of faith, believing in Christ's work on the cross and shedding His blood to wash away their sins. Both see it as dying to self, buried with Christ and then being raised to new life.

I was in for another surprise this morning as I turned to read my devotional <u>My Utmost for His Highest</u> by Oswald Chambers. What perfect timing as he explained "justification by faith" on October 28. Another one of "God's Divine timing" in helping me explain "Taking the first step" of salvation.

In essence, Oswald Chambers states that it is not repentance that saves us but repentance is the sign that we realize what God has done through Jesus Christ. We are made right with God because Christ died for us. When we turn to God and accept by faith what God has now revealed to us, the miraculous atonement by the cross of Christ instantly places me in right relationship with God. As a result of the supernatural miracle of God's grace we stand "justified", not because we are sorry for our sin or because we have repented, but because of what Jesus has done! The Spirit of God brings justification with a shattering, radiant light, and we know we are saved, even though we don't know how it was accomplished.

In John 1:29, Jesus Christ came to take away the sin of the world. Christ died on the cross for us while we were still living in sin (Romans 5:8). By accepting Jesus' death on the cross for our sins, we are being totally forgiven and set free from our life of sin. We are "saved" from total separation from God by the acceptance of Jesus' death on the cross. Salvation is free but it was not cheap and we cannot earn it by our good works.

Let me interject here that we often think that God saved us from our sin of lying, cheating, anger, physical abuse, stealing, murder and all the other things we may have done. But in all reality, our sin has been the rejection of Christ and what He did on the cross for us. I believe that when a person stands before God on Judgement Day that God is not going to ask them about all the things they did wrong on earth. I truly believe God will only ask one question, "What did you do with My Son Jesus who died on the cross for you?"

We will never be worthy of Christ's forgiveness. It's a free gift! In Romans 6:23 it says *For the wages of sin is death, but the **gift** of God is eternal life through Jesus Christ our Lord (emphasis added)*. We can't earn eternal life. We need to accept Jesus love and forgiveness and thank Him for giving His life as a sacrifice for our sin. Confessing Jesus as Lord and inviting Him to be in control of our life is the beginning of a wonderful relationship with God, Jesus and the Holy Spirit. Romans 10:13 says that *whoever calls on the name of the Lord shall be saved*. But that is just the beginning of an exciting walk with Jesus!

Granted, there are people who say they believe in God, but so does the devil and his demons, and they tremble as we read in

James 2:19. Just believing in a God will not get you to heaven. There are also people who study the Bible and can quote scripture, but they do not have a personal relationship with the Author God. We can only begin this adventure of knowing the living God by simply asking Him to forgive us, and allow that forgiveness to change us.

There are some people who are the most honest people you will ever meet. They are the nicest people and they may even attend church. They obey the laws of the land and are people you can look up to and admire. That person may be one of those that do not feel that they need God in their lives. They are doing just great and everything may be going well for them in life at this time.

However, the root of all sin is pride and you may not see it in yourself. When I'm teaching I start writing the word "pride" at the bottom of the white board and then sin above it, since pride is the root of sin. Then I continue to write more words above them showing what Christ has done for us, because that is the direction God brings us is "up to Him". The devil or enemy wants to "take us down". So, as you read the following words please start with the word PRIDE at the bottom and continue reading up to the word obedience.

OBED-I-ENCE
AL-I-VE
H-I-S
D-I-E
PR-I-CE
CRUC-I-FIED
SACR-I-FICE
S-I-N
PR-I-DE

Did you see that the letter "I" is right in the center of pride and sin? Before Christ it is usually all about me, self-centered and self-focused. I don't need God. Also notice that Jesus was the ultimate sacrifice for "I", yes me. He was crucified for "I" and paid the price for "I" so He had to die for "I", yes me. Now because of H-I-S death for "I", He has made me AL-I-VE in Him so my spirit is now born again.

Christ was obedient to the Heavenly Father in the garden the night before He was crucified in Mark 14:36 and Luke 22:42. He prayed for the heavenly Father to take this cup (of suffering and death on the cross) from Him but then He said, *never the less, Your will be done.* Remember, Jesus was human. It was not easy for Him to face the beating and torture, then be nailed to a cross for our sins. H-I-S obedience was again for "I", yes for (I) me, right in the center. In 1 Corinthians 7:23 we read that we were bought at (or with) a price! He paid the ultimate PR-I-CE for you too.

When we surrender to the Lord we choose to walk in obedience to Him. Notice that the word DIE is in the middle of OBE-DIE-NCE? We have to DIE to "I", yes, die to self so we can walk in OBEDIENCE to our Lord and Savior Jesus Christ. By walking in obedience doesn't mean following man-made laws, religion and traditions of men, it means growing in love with Jesus. As you grow in your knowledge of Him by reading the Bible the Holy Spirit will guide you and direct you. If you are doing something not pleasing to the Lord you will be convicted of that. The Holy Spirit is also our Comforter and Guide because Jesus set us free to walk in joy and freedom.

The Bible uses the word flesh in Galatians 5:16-24, *I say then: Walk in the Spirit, and you shall not fulfill the lusts of the flesh.* The Spirit and the flesh oppose each other. The flesh refers to everything in a person that opposes God and His will in our lives. Interestingly enough as you read verse 24 it states *And those who are Christ's have crucified the flesh with its passions and desire.* That means we have to die to self and lay aside thoughts, desires and actions that are not pleasing to God and walk in a manner that represents Jesus Christ.

Can you see the triangle below that forms between the Father, the Son and the Holy Spirit? Please draw the triangle now and write GOD in the center. Do you see the triangle between the body, soul and spirit? Please draw the triangle now and write your name in the middle.

Father   Body

————————   ————————

Son   Holy Spirit   Soul   spirit

Please note that the Holy Spirit is in capital letters but the spirit of man is in small case when you read the scriptures. In 1 Thessalonians 5:23 it reads, *Now may the God of peace Himself sanctify you* (**set you apart**) *completely; and may your whole spirit, soul and body, be preserved blameless at the coming of our Lord Jesus Christ (emphasis added).*

Regarding the "spirit", like I said earlier we are made up of 3 parts just like the Divine Trinity; we have a spirit, soul and body. When a person accepts the forgiveness that Christ offers then their spirit is born again from above and they are a new creation in Christ Jesus according to 2 Corinthians 5:17 *Therefore, if anyone is in Christ, he is a new creation; old things have passed away; behold, all things have become new.*

Now regarding the "soul", it is made up of 3 parts, the MIND or intellect, the WILL and the EMOTIONS. Before accepting Christ the spirit of man is dead (the word "man" in the Bible refers to man or woman) and they are trying to figure God out with their "MIND" or intellect and the Bible doesn't make any sense to them. Their mind has not yet been renewed by the Spirit and by the Word of God, the Bible.

That is why the story of the cross and Jesus is foolishness to the non-believers in 1 Corinthians 2:14. People make fun of

38

Christians and say we need a crutch so we get "religion". Oh my friend, religion is the greatest tool of the enemy, the devil, who condemns us and makes a person feel like they have to get their life in order before they can come to Jesus. Religion is bondage but Jesus Christ sets us free from sin and bondage.

Before a person comes to Christ their "WILL" chooses to do whatever they want, anytime they want and can choose to please that person in life. When a person is born again from above by the Holy Spirit, their will is now to please the Lord and make choices that reflect Christ in their life.

The third part of the "soul" has to do with "EMOTIONS". Before Christ it is easy to submit to whatever emotions are affecting them. If the person gets upset they can verbally or physically abuse someone. They can let their emotions control them in whatever way their "flesh" or "self" wants to exhibit their emotions. Emotions can be good or bad depending on how one controls them. With Christ in our life, our will changes and it helps us to control our emotions much better. No we are not perfect, we can still make mistakes because we are still growing and changing to be more Christ-like in our walk with God. But the Spirit is now working in us.

Regarding the "body", a person will not go to heaven if they have not asked Christ to forgive their sins and submitted their life to Christ. God is able, through the Holy Spirit, to make changes in their habits and life styles. God can and does deliver people from addictions, which is anything that controls a person. When I ask someone if they know where they will go when they die, they normally say, "I hope I go to heaven". There is no confidence or assurance of that because they do not understand what Christ has done for them.

I want to stop here and let you have an opportunity to accept the forgiveness that Christ offers you if you have never done that before. It is so simple and yet so powerful what God will do in your life. I have covered everything you need to know, now it is just a matter of your having faith in God for what He has accomplished through His Son Jesus on the Cross. I am sure you have heard this verse or seen it at parades or football games multiple times in your life, John 3:16 *For God so loved the world that He gave His only begotten Son, that whoever believes in Him should not perish but have everlasting life.* Just say these words out loud if you can, or at least under your breath where you can hear yourself say it.

Jesus, I believe that You died on the cross and shed your blood for my sins. I also believe that You were raised from the dead and You went to heaven so You could send the Holy Spirit. Please forgive me for not acknowledging You before and living my life with no regard for You. I accept Your love and Your forgiveness. Thank You for making me new inside and giving me eternal life. Thank you for the things that You are starting to work out of my life now and for what You are going to work into my life by the power of Your Holy Spirit. Thank You Jesus, I'm now born again and I'm a child of God.

Dear friend, the Holy Spirit is now working in your life. You are born again of the Spirit. It is important that you share with others that you just asked Jesus Christ to come into your life. There is power in confessing Jesus as your Savior! That is also why it is good if you were able to pray those words out loud. But if you were not able to do that, please share your decision with others every chance you get. That will help confirm it in your heart and spirit. It will also help you keep your commitment to Jesus, as it is like "keeping your word" when you promised to meet someone for lunch.

Speaking that prayer out loud results in you hearing your own words and confession of faith. You have heard the Word of God, you have believed and you have stepped out in faith to receive this free gift of salvation. Please realize that as you share your decision with others that some may rejoice with you and others may not understand or make fun of you. Do not let that bother you, Christ was also made fun of and not understood. Be kind and loving in your responses to them.

Here are some instructions to help you in your new walk with Christ. Being baptized in water is a command of Jesus as I covered in Matthew 28:19-20. Make every effort to find a good solid Bible teaching church and ask to be baptized in water unless you gave your life to Christ in a church that has you baptized at the same time.

Purchase a Holy Bible so you can start getting to know more about your Lord and Savior Jesus Christ. I highly recommend The Spirit Filled Bible and you can get it in a very easy reading style like the New International Version (NIV). I really like my New King James Version and I love giving people this Bible.

I encourage you to get involved in a small group at that church where people are doing Bible studies or your church may have special Bible studies. We need to be in fellowship and friendship with other Christians so we can grow. In church you will be taught about the Bible and about God. In the small groups you can grow and get to know people who will pray for each other. You have instantly become a part of the family of God when you gave your life to Christ.

You will find that there are no perfect Christians in this world, as God is working on all of us. If you ever have any thoughts that you are not saved and you were just emotional when you prayed, then put that thought out of your mind and say out loud, "Thank you Jesus for saving me and for keeping me now even though I do not feel saved, I'm a believer and I'm saved by faith!"

At this time I'm going to share more about this process of salvation in hopes that it will even make it clearer and give you greater understandings of our spiritual lives and our walk with Christ. These are things I have learned over the years.

There are three steps I refer to as the process of salvation. First, in John 3:3 we repent of living our life our way and we are born again of the "Spirit" which means we are now saved or

41

have "salvation". Second, in Philippians 2:12-13, we work out our salvation in our "soul" which means God begins to show us things that do not please Him and how to live like Him. In turn, we begin to be more Christ-like in our choices, life and actions. As a result we are in the process of "sanctification", or being set apart from the world and sin. The third step is found in II Corinthians 1:9-10, allowing Christ to work in our "body". He delivers us from old habits or addictions and prepares us to reflect Him more in our lives. Then when we die we will go to heaven and have a glorified body.

When our spirit is born again or made new at salvation, we are "set apart" from the world and we are "sanctified" and "Justified". We have been cleansed from sin and we are now "Just-as-if-id" never sinned. In Romans 5:1, *Therefore, having been justified by faith, we have peace with God through our Lord Jesus Christ,* which basically means "declared righteous". Please read Romans 5:9-11 and 8:30, then read 1 Corinthians 6:11 to see that when we submit our lives to Jesus that we are "washed", "sanctified" and "justified". Thank you Lord.

When you receive the salvation offered to you by the shedding of Christ's blood on the cross for your sins then you are "baptized into Christ by the Spirit". Galatians 3:26-28 reads *For you are all sons of God through faith in Jesus Christ. For as many of you as were baptized into Christ have put on Christ. There is neither Jew, nor Greek, there is neither slave, or free, there is neither male, nor female; for you are all one in Christ Jesus.* Is that awesome? No matter where we live on earth or what language we speak, we are born again brothers and sisters in Christ being in the family of God.

I think there are two parts to sanctification. The first is when your spirit is born again at the time of salvation and you are "set apart", sanctified or justified. The second part is when our "soul" starts growing in Christ and we are in the process of "sanctification" or being "set apart" from the world in a greater

42

and deeper way. Jesus who was our offering in Hebrews 10:14 *...has perfected forever those who are being sanctified.*

As we grow in the Lord by reading the Word, then the Holy Spirit starts to change our desires so we don't care to watch, read or do some of things we did before. Those things didn't bother us before even if they weren't major things. He keeps drawing us to the Father and the things of this world no longer have the pull on us so we start wanting more of Him.

We don't want to be conformed to this world so our "mind" is being renewed by the Word and by the Spirit. As a result our thinking is changing as we see in Romans 12:1-2 *I beseech you therefore, brethren, by the mercies of God, that you present your bodies a living sacrifice, holy, acceptable to God, which is your reasonable service. And do not be conformed to this world, but be transformed by the renewing of your mind, that you may prove what is that good and acceptable and perfect will of God.* We can actually make good choices by being in our "right mind" now with God's help.

Our will is changing and our emotions don't rule us. Our body is being set free from bad habits and addictions. We are new creations in Christ Jesus. When we die we will go to heaven and receive a new body. Or it may happen at the rapture of the church when Jesus comes to take us to heaven we will receive our new glorified bodies.

Can you see our three parts more clearly now as I display them below. As I see it, this is the process of salvation.

Spirit	Soul	Body
Salvation	Sanctification	Glorification
"Have been saved"	"Being saved"	"Will be saved"

In Ephesians 2:8 it says that we *have been saved.* I totally understood that when I came to Jesus.

When it says we are *"being saved"* in 1 Corinthians 1:18, it is referring to our soul and the process of growing deeper in sanctification. I have learned over the years, I'm still "being saved" (from my flesh) as I'm "working out my salvation". In Philippians 2:12-13, it reads *...work out your own salvation with fear and trembling; for it is God who works in you both to will and to do for His good pleasure.*

God keeps revealing areas in my life that I need to surrender to Him to be more like Jesus. As long as I'm alive, He is still helping me to "work out my salvation". I'm still growing and I do not know it all!

When the scripture says I *"will be saved"* in 1 Corinthians 3:15, I didn't understand that before. What? I will be saved? No, I was already saved! But Paul is not talking about salvation; he is talking about our body. Our body will be saved at the rapture or coming of Christ. Remember that when we take our last breath and die here on earth, like Paul says in 2 Corinthians 5:8, *to be absent in the body is to be present with the Lord.* Our spirit will be with the Lord the moment after we draw our last breath.

However, if we are alive when Jesus comes, what we call the rapture (a snatching away) we will be taken to heaven. The word rapture is not in the Bible but Jesus will be coming back to snatch us away quickly. In 1 Thessalonians 4:16-18 it reads *For the Lord Himself will descend from heaven with a shout, with the voice of an archangel, and with the trumpet of God. And the dead in Christ will rise first. Then we who are alive and remain shall be caught up together with them in the clouds to meet the Lord in the air. And thus we shall always be with the Lord. Therefore comfort one another with these words.*

Paul writes in Hebrews 6:1-2, that he didn't want to start discussing all the basic foundations or essentials of belief but he wanted to go on and teach on deeper things. He just mentioned the basic doctrines including the "doctrine of baptisms" as one of those essential foundations but did not feel he had to teach on it again. I see the doctrine of baptisms that he mentions as a 3 part work of the Spirit.

As I previously mentioned the first doctrine of baptisms is being "baptized into Christ by the Spirit" as we just read in Galatians 3:26-28. The second doctrine is when we are "baptized in water by a person" like John did the baptizing for repentance in Mark 1:8. John also baptized Jesus to be obedient to the Scripture in Matthew 3:13-17. The third doctrine is the "baptism in the Holy Spirit" that we read in Matthew 3:11, *He will baptize you in the Holy Spirit and fire* speaking of Jesus as the baptizer. This baptism in the Holy Spirit took place on the Day of Pentecost in Acts 2:4.

When a person gets saved the Holy Spirit starts to work in us but He doesn't "CONTROL" us. Does that raise the hair on the back of your neck? I know some will disagree with me but keep reading. I believe He helps us, comforts us, reminds us, draws us, and comes along side of us. He also brings us peace as it talks about the fruit of the Spirit in Galatians 5:22.

In Philippians 2:5 it states, *Let this mind be in you which was also in Christ Jesus.* I believe we have the freedom of choice since the word "let" is used here for example. Now allow me tell you what "CONTROL" means as I have learned it.

A young couple came to Christ when they were in the Bakersfield, California jail. When they moved to Fresno they attended our church. I noticed they did more "watching" us as we were singing and worshipping. After several months they started entering into worship. I got to know him and he explained to me that they both had been involved in the occult. They had been taking blood baths and other things I won't mention in their satanic worship. He said they were under the "control" of demonic spirits and did things they had no control over. When they came to Christ he was very leery (or scared) of being under the "control" of another spirit. He said the "spirit realm" is very real, whether it is the Holy Spirit or demonic spirits. He said that he has learned that the Holy Spirit is not a "controlling" Spirit because the Holy Spirit sets us free to have a choice to serve God.

Now, let me share my thinking. The Holy Spirit doesn't "control" me otherwise I would be a robot. However, because I love the Lord and I choose to be obedient to the Holy Spirit's promptings I want to be submissive to Him. That means, I "choose" to submit to the Lord, I "choose" to be led of the Spirit and I want to give him total "CONTROL" of my life. It is a matter of choice. I want Jesus to be "LORD" of my life and I want to have the mind of Christ! The meaning of "Lordship" is allowing Jesus to rule and reign in my mind, my will and my emotions which includes my finances and every area of my life. Yes I know that God is in control of this world okay? I also know that God is in control of my life and nothing will happen to me without His approval. He will be my guide and my source as long as I look to Him, love Him and serve Him.

The Holy Spirit is a gentleman. So who do you want to sit on the throne of your life? If you want to rule your own life then the Holy Spirit will not push His way up on the throne. If you want the Spirit to be on the throne of your life, you do well and you will see growth in your spiritual journey. But if that temptation comes to get angry at someone or do something that is not pleasing to the Lord, the Holy Spirit will step off the throne and allow your flesh to rule and reign.

I have found that the Holy Spirit will quietly check my spirit when a thought comes to my mind that is not Christ-like. He gives me a chance to obey the Spirit before the flesh can take over. However, if I yield to the temptation, He steps off the throne of my life and lets me do as I want. The Lord wants us to serve Him with a whole heart and let the Holy Spirit guide and direct our lives. I do not believe the Holy Spirit will make us do anything against our will.

What a joy to be born again and not have to be concerned about our past sins as they are covered in the blood of Jesus. Of course, if we have broken any laws or done wrong things we will have to suffer the consequences for our prior actions and possibly make restitution. But as far as Jesus is concerned, you may be in jail but you are free inside!

My father-in-law had a saying that when God forgives you He puts up a sign at the "Sea of Forgiveness" where He buried your sins and the sign says "NO FISHING ALLOWED". The past is the past so don't go back there! Let it go. God gives us a clean slate on the chalkboard of life because of what Jesus did on the cross so we are totally clean and forgiven.

Of course it doesn't hurt to glance back in the rear view mirror and remember where God has brought you from so you can give Him thanks. But keep your eyes on the road ahead to see where God is taking you.

It is good to remember what Paul said to the church at Philippi. In Philippians 3:12-14 *Brethren, I do not count myself to have apprehended; but one thing I do, forgetting those things which are behind and reaching forward to those things which are ahead, I press toward the goal for the prize of the upward call of God in Christ Jesus.* Paul said he wasn't perfect and he does not know it all but he was pressing forward in his walk with Christ Jesus! I like that as I relate to that for sure!

I watched a young 19 year old sharing this at his youth group meeting recently that someone had captured on their phone video and it is powerful. He told the youth group: "You can't go back and change the beginning, but you can start right where you are right now and you can change the ending."

CHAPTER 5
A HUNGER FOR MORE

Do you have a hunger to know Jesus more and to understand His ways? Just because you are reading this book I believe that you do have a hunger and thirst for more of Him.

In Jeremiah 9:23-24, God is speaking and states that we are not to boast (or glory) in our wisdom, not to boast in our might and not to boast in our riches, *'But let him who glories glory in this that he understands and knows Me, that I am the LORD, exercising lovingkindness, judgement and righteousness in the earth. For in these I delight,' says the LORD.* He delights in us knowing Him and understanding Him. After I memorized these scriptures I have seen those two words "understands and knows" jumping off the pages of the Bible often when I'm reading it.

In Matthew 5:6 it reads *Blessed are those who hunger and thirst for righteousness, for they shall be filled.* What is righteousness? Basically it means the quality of being morally right or justifiable. In other words it is being in right standing with God. Then filled with what? More of Him? More of Jesus who is righteous? Could it be if we hunger and thirst for righteousness that we could be filled up with more of Jesus?

In Psalm 63:1-8. It states, *Oh God, You are my God, early will I seek You.* That shows there is a hunger for Him! I have to make a choice to get up early to seek His face and spend time with Him. That hunger and desire comes from the heart. Fortunately I have been a morning person so getting up early was easy for me. If you are not a morning person that is okay, God created you different. Just find a good quiet time that you can spend with Jesus in the Word, worshipping and in prayer. When I use the word worshipping I mean singing and maybe playing an instrument if you can, as well as speaking thanks and praise to the Lord out loud.

Then it continues to read, *My soul thirsts for you*; and whenever I read SOUL in the Bible I always think "MIND, WILL AND EMOTIONS", which makes it simpler for me to understand. I read it like this, "My mind, will and emotions thirsts for you". I need a drink of the Spirit in my life every day. The verse continues, *My flesh longs for you in a dry and thirsty land where there is no water.*

Now that is a picture of being in the desert with nothing to drink. My flesh and bones are parched and crying out for one drop of water on my tongue. That is a picture of how thirsty I am for more of the Lord! Friend, I hope you are thirsty for more of Jesus. In John 7:37-39 Jesus said, '*If anyone thirsts, let him come to Me and drink. He who believes in Me, as the Scripture has said, out of his heart will flow rivers of living water.' But this He spoke concerning the Spirit, whom those believing in Him would receive; for the Holy Spirit was not yet given, because Jesus was not yet glorified.*

I want to encourage you to seek a deeper relationship with Jesus! Spend time in His presence. When you read the Word and pray, take time to start communicating with the Lord. Most of our praying has a tendency to ask God for things. Instead, start being still and just listen when you finish your devotions or "quiet time" with the Lord. He will start speaking to your spirit and bring thoughts to your mind also.

If I say meditate on the Lord I do not mean like Yoga. You can be sitting, walking, standing or in any position as you just focus your mind on Jesus and His love for you. When I am traveling alone I have such a wonderful time in the car singing and praising the Lord! You are a child of the King of Kings, you can talk to your heavenly Father anytime and you can learn to listen to what He wants to say to you. I also discovered I can ask the Lord questions and He will answer me. In John 10:27 Jesus said, '*My sheep hear My voice, and I know them, and they follow Me*'.

This is something I had to learn to do. What I have learned and understand is that the Holy Spirit speaks to our "born again" spirit. Then our spirit brings that thought to our mind. There are so many scriptures about our mind. The main one I repeat is Philippians 2:5, *Let this mind be in you, which was also in Christ Jesus.* In Romans 12:1-2 It reads *I beseech you therefore brethren, by the mercies of God, that you present your bodies a living sacrifice, holy, acceptable to God, which is your reasonable service. And do not be conformed to this world, but be transformed by the renewing of your mind, that you may prove what is that good and perfect and acceptable will of God.*

Again, I can't say that I can prove it in the Bible that the Holy Spirit speaks to our spirit and then brings that thought to our mind but other people who love the Lord have shared the same thinking and experiences. It sure makes sense to me and that is what I have experienced in my life since I do not hear His audible voice.

I tried to keep my do to list in my brain as I was reading my Bible. It was so hard to concentrate on what the Bible was saying to me. I was so legalistic I felt it was a sin to have my planner with my Bible. I finally realized it was not a sin to write my "to do list" while having time with the Lord. If I remembered that I had to go to the bank, I wrote it down, forgot about it and went back to reading my Bible. I was at peace then and my mind was focused right back on the Bible.

When I finished worshipping, praying and being in the Word, I learned to be still in His presence. Thoughts then came to me to write to my friend John in prison or go visit Gary in the memory care home so I wrote it down in my planner.

For many years I would end my devotional time and say, "Lord I give You permission to interrupt my day anytime You want to". Not that He needs my permission, but it showed Him my heart and attitude and that I wanted to be submissive to His leading my steps through the day. It is a choice, because I want the Spirit to be control of my life. Oh yes, He has interrupted me more than once and I was able to pray for people, lead someone to the Lord, and witness or encourage someone. No I don't always get my "TO DO LIST" done, but I sure want to obey His voice and get His "TO DO LIST" done!

You might say that doesn't sound like God telling me to write to John in prison, or to go see Gary, or call someone. Maybe it was just me and my own thoughts, or maybe it was the Lord directing me as I wrote the letter to encourage John. Maybe it was the Lord when I saw Gary and shared with him, read the Word and prayed with him. But even if it was "just me", did it hurt to do those things? I'd rather fail trying to be obedient to the Holy Spirit, than to not obey at all and just question those thoughts that come to my mind.

Another example of hearing the Holy Spirit communicate with me was when the thought came to my mind "Call Ken and share with him what you are reading in the Bible right now". So I stopped and I called Ken right away. I said, "Ken I'm reading in _____ and you came to my mind". I don't have to say, "Ken, I was reading in _____ and God spoke to me and said to call you". When I told Ken where I was reading and that he came to my mind, Ken said, "Jerry that is the exact scriptures the Lord has been speaking to me all week".

Now do you think that was "just me"? That was a word of encouragement and confirmation for Ken that he was hearing the Lord. It also built my faith and encouraged me to keep listening for the Holy Spirit to speak to me. I wrote Ken's name and the date by that scripture in my Bible and I have sent a picture of that page to him once or twice since then. It is good to be reminded of what the Lord has done for us or has spoken to us.

As you spend time in the Word and desiring to know Him more, He will start revealing things to you in the Bible so that it becomes alive to you. You look forward to your time alone in the Word and with Jesus praying and worshipping. When I finish spending my time alone with Jesus and I step outside I'm looking for opportunities to share Jesus with someone or to pray for someone. I'm hungry for Jesus to use me, to touch someone's life for the kingdom.

Adults can have more difficulty accepting this teaching because of their intellect. We want to figure things out and understand everything about a matter before we accept it. It may sound strange to you to hear me say that you can "hear the Lord's voice". Let me share with you some ways to hear His voice that I have experienced. Remember that I'm still growing in my walk with the Lord and I'm still learning also.

In your desire to have a hunger for more of the Holy Spirit working in your life, never forget that the main way that the Holy Spirit speaks to us is through the Bible, His holy Word. As we read the Bible He can bring things to our attention to open our eyes to something we need to know. The Holy Spirit is the author and He may give us direction or correction as we read in 2 Timothy 3:16 *All Scripture is given by inspiration of God, and is profitable for doctrine, for reproof, for correction, for instruction in righteousness, that the man of God may be complete, thoroughly equipped for every good work.*

We do not earn our salvation or our close relationship with the Lord by doing good works. However, because of our relationship with Jesus we have a servant's heart like Jesus and we show the world our faith in God by our good works as it reads in James 2:14–26.

Another example is from Pastor Mike Robertson who wrote a book called "The God Nudge". It is an excellent source and very helpful as it was written in an easy to read manner. In essence, the God nudge is that little prompting of the Holy Spirit to do something or say something.

For example, one morning the thought came to me and I wrote down in my planner to go and see Jane in the Assisted Living complex. On the way to see Jane I was just "prompted" to turn left on a different street instead of taking my normal route. No I didn't "hear God" speak to me, I had no "Holy Ghost goose bumps" like some people have said. It was just a very brief thought or idea to turn left so I did. I say a "thought" but really I didn't even have time to think about it, I just had this quick, brief idea to turn left.

Two blocks down the street I saw a young man on crutches going as fast as he could. A thought came to me that I needed to go back and offer him a ride so I backed up real fast and offered him a ride. He was very thankful since he had a dentist appointment 5 miles away. I started talking to him about the Lord and by the time we arrived he was weeping and he accepted Jesus in his life.

I gave him my business card and counseled him in his new walk with Jesus. Was that the Lord or was that just my idea to turn left on that street? I totally believe it was a "God nudge". I never thought about turning, there was no time to ponder or discuss the pros and cons about going a different way. Then when I saw the man the Holy Spirit put a thought in my mind to pick him up. Do you see the difference in the God nudge and the thoughts the Holy Spirit can bring to our mind? You are learning to hear His voice when you realize those thoughts are being brought to your mind by your spirit as the Holy Spirit gives them to you.

Jack Deere talks about the "internal audible voice" which is very different and very unique that I have also experienced. There have been at least 7 or more specific times when the Lord by His Holy Spirit has spoken to me by that internal audible voice. It was clear and concise when He gave me correction, direction or peace of mind. In your walk with Jesus you will hear that special voice or it might be a whisper to you.

Sitting in the plane in Fresno I was waiting to fly to North Carolina to see my two brothers. I planned to fly on a Friday so I could spend the weekend with them and report to Washington D.C. Headquarters for a briefing on Monday morning. I was reading my One Year Bible that has a portion to read in the Old Testament, the Psalms, Proverbs and in the New Testament each day. I had this awesome idea to read ahead a couple days since I would not have time to read my Bible on Saturday or Sunday morning because I would get up early and visit all day. So I opened my Bible and before I could even start to read the Holy Spirit spoke so very loud and clear in that "internal audible voice" and said to me, "*You can't gather up the manna!*"

That was a word of warning and reminder that we must have fresh manna every day, and the manna is the Word of God that is also called the "bread of life". Just like in the wilderness the children of Israel had to pick up the manna every morning to eat for nourishment. In fact, when they saved it up for the next day the manna would have worms and stink as we read in Exodus 16:15-32. I can't save up the Word by reading ahead. I need fresh bread from heaven on a daily basis in my life. Jesus said in John 6:35 *I am the bread of life*...So on Saturday and Sunday morning, I stayed in my bedroom until I had my time in the Word, prayer and with Jesus before I would come out to visit with my brothers.

In 1997 I was working my first Private Investigator case. Barbara and I normally walked 3 miles early in the morning and prayed together. After that, we spent our time alone with the Lord when we got home. On that Friday morning when we got home from our prayer walk, I decided to go look for an individual. His parents in New Mexico thought he may have been critically hurt or killed by drug dealers since they had not heard from him in weeks and his rental car had not been turned in. I thought I would be back by 9:00am and then have time with the Lord.

Fast forward, it was 9:30 at night and I was still trying to find this guy. As I drove home the Holy Spirit spoke to me in that "internal audible voice" and said so very loud and clear "*If you don't spend time with Me first, you are wasting your time"*. I said, "Lord I'm so sorry, I know better, I'm sorry you had to remind me."

The next morning Barbara and I walked and prayed, and then I spent my time with Jesus. I didn't get out of the house until 8:30 and I thought the guy probably already left the motel or left town if he was still alive. At 9:15 I saw a bank open where someone had been taking money out of his bank account. I was surprised the bank was open on Saturday morning so I went inside hoping to find out who was using his bank account and making withdrawals.

Identifying myself to the bank manager and showing her a picture of the person, I told her I was looking for this person and explained why. I wanted to know who was taking money out of his bank account at different locations including this one. She said, "Oh, he was here yesterday at 4:00 PM to withdraw some cash. He lost his wallet and has to come into the bank to make a withdrawal. By the way we close at noon and I will no longer be here at this bank".

Does God know what He is doing? Can He solve a case? When I do what I need to do by putting Him first in my life every day I always get more accomplished. I was able to call the parents and tell them that their son was alive. I told them the whole story of what happened to me and how I found the information to give God the glory. But there is still more to this story!

Okay, here is one of those "weird" things that the Holy Spirit can do, but there is a big difference when the Holy Spirit does it opposed to when a person does something real weird out of their "feelings" or "emotions". I will cover that topic more in the chapter titled "Ugly". That next Monday I set up a surveillance at 11:00 a.m. at that same bank in Fresno even though he was supposed to be working in Sequoia National Park east of Visalia, about 90 miles away. Is that weird or what? That doesn't make any logical sense! I just had that thought come to me to do it like that.

At 11:21 AM, my partner assisting me on the surveillance radioed me from the bank parking lot where he was stationed, and told me that the person just drove up and was going into the bank. I got to the bank and stopped him as he was walking out. I told him his parents were worried about him and I took him to a phone booth and he called them. I also had my partner take a picture of us standing by his car and I sent the photo to his parents. Case solved! In 25 years of being a federal agent, there has never been a 21 minute surveillance.

Thank the Lord I spent time with Him on that Monday morning and I listened to the Holy Spirit as He directed me how to set up that surveillance. It really didn't make sense, but it worked! That was a perfect example of being "led of the Spirit" because in my normal way of thinking, that was a very stupid idea and made no sense at all. That could be classed as something "weird" by some people but the Holy Spirit didn't embarrass me or Himself!

If God can speak to me and use me, because I am no one special, he can use you! As you desire to know Him more and you spend time in the Word, sharing your heart with Jesus, then He will begin speaking to your spirit. He will bring thoughts to your mind and whisper to you when you need it. How wonderful that we have a personal God and Holy Spirit that wants to communicate with us! Be faithful and commit your heart to knowing him as you hunger for more of Jesus!

Some people have had bad experiences at church or have heard wild and crazy things about the baptism in the Holy Spirit. That is so sad because the baptism in the Holy Spirit totally changed my walk with God. I never prayed for anyone to accept Jesus before that experience and I never had the boldness or faith to pray for someone for their healing. I was never used to touch a life like the Lord has used me since that day on February 11, 1973. It is so exciting to walk in the Spirit day by day.

I remember hearing a preacher say "A person must be open and hungry for more of the Lord to receive the baptism in the Holy Spirit. The purpose of the baptism in the Holy Spirit is to have power to evangelize the world, not just to speak in tongues". To that I say "Amen!"

Our walk with God is our choice. I have said that, "God will be just as close to us as we will let Him". In James 4:8 it reads, *Draw near to God and He will draw near to you.* Psalm 25:4-5 is encouraging as it reads *Show me Your ways oh Lord, teach me Your paths, lead me in Your truth and teach me, for You are the God of my salvation, on You I wait all the day.* As I have memorized and meditated on this verse, I see the importance of having a heart and mind that "waits on Him". He will lead me in His truth and teach me step by step.

I want to commend you if you are following Jesus. That is a good thing. Here is a stick man to represent Jesus with a person who is following in Jesus footsteps.

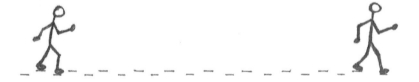

The question is, how hungry are you to "know Him"? How close are you to Jesus? Are you keeping up with Jesus? Are you close enough to hear His voice? I hope you are!

My concern is that if a person is following Jesus but they are not close enough to hear Him, how can they be obedient to His voice or prompting by the Holy Spirit? What if something takes their attention from Jesus and they can end up going down a wrong path or getting sidetracked. It may not be a bad thing, or it may be a very bad temptation that will cause them to lose total sight of Jesus in their life.

Look at the following picture I drew. You may want to stop and analyze it because you could miss something.

If we are not close to the Lord on a daily basis, our minds can start focusing on other things. What about that girl? Or are we fixated on a cool car? Is it money and wealth? It is easy to go off on another path especially if those footprints are fading in the sand as you can see in my sketch. Did you see the footprints fading? Are you walking so far behind Jesus that you might wake up one day and you won't be able to see Him at all? What a frightening thought!

In Psalm 63:8 it reads *My soul* (my mind, my will and my emotions) ***follows close behind You*** (emphasis added). In other words, I'm staying close to Jesus and keeping my mind and focus on Him. My will is to do His will, and I will not let my emotions control me. It's great if you're following that close to Jesus. The verse continues to say *Your right hand upholds me.* I can see you walking so close behind Jesus that His right hand is reaching back as your following Him. He is holding your hand and "upholding you" so you won't stumble or fall as He guides you down the pathway of life. That is a very good place to be.

How much more intimate do you think it would be to walk in step "with Jesus", so close to Him that nothing comes between you and Him? Now, that's what I'm talking about! My heart cry and prayer over this book is that we would all desire to "walk with Jesus"! Oh that we walk so close to Him that we are in step with Him feeling His heartbeat and hear His whisper as shown in my sketch below.

If you are hungry for more of Jesus, He will take you to places where you can grow in Him. He may take you to some places that may not feel good. He may let you feel like you're walking alone for a season without feeling His presence. This is a test...this is only a test!

In John chapter 6, Jesus was looking at the large multitude of people and in verse 5 Jesus asked Philip where they could buy bread to feed all of them. In verse 6 it reads *But this He said to test him, for He Himself knew what He would do.* That is where the 5000 men were fed with 5 barley loaves and 2 fish with 12 baskets left over, not counting women and children.

By the way, did you realize that Jesus didn't feed the multitude? After Jesus gave thanks and blessed it then it multiplied for the 12 disciples. Then it multiplied again as the 12 disciples fed 5,000 men, and even more women and children. When God blesses something He makes it multiply and God uses imperfect people like us to minister to others. He was testing Philip's faith. As we mature in the Lord we know we can trust Him because He has proven Himself trustworthy over and over again. God gives the increase and He also has leftovers so we can share some more with others.

In Jeremiah 20:12 it states, *Oh LORD of hosts, You who test the righteous, and see the mind and heart* (most secret place). But He will never leave you and never forsake you when you are tested. There may come a time you will need to walk by faith for a season, learning to trust Him. I've been there and done that. He wants you to grow and it can be a challenging but enriching season in your life if you don't give up as you're learning to trust Him.

In the middle of the 1970's I experienced a 6 month dry spell when I didn't feel Gods presence. I would literally cry to feel His presence. My brother Ralph called me from Arizona and encouraged me to worship and praise Him. As foreign as that sounds when you don't feel like praising God, do it anyway because there is power in praise. Praising God when you are in a trial or you don't feel Him is called a sacrifice of praise. At that time when I didn't even "feel" anything, I followed what it reads in Hebrews 13:15, *Therefore by Him let us continually offer the sacrifice of praise to God, that is, the fruit of our lips, giving thanks to His name.* If you are in that season of testing and growing now, I encourage you to stop and make a list of things that you can be grateful for. Begin with your very breath. Can you dress yourself, can you walk and feed yourself? Add to your list everything you can think of, and then start giving God thanks and praise!

When I looked back at that time of my life, I realized it was just a test. During former times of ministry I would pray with people to accept Christ or pray with them at the altar in church and I always told them not to worry about their feelings. I told them that they must ask Jesus into their life by faith. I told them to think about their relationship with God as though it was a train, Jesus is the engine, their faith is the coal car and their feelings are the caboose. You may not feel God's presence one day, and the newness of your experience with the Lord may "feel" very different. That is because you are allowing the caboose to run your train! Don't trust the caboose, you can unhook it and your train will keep moving forward.

So my friend, don't worry about your feelings and don't let your feelings control you. The enemy will come and try to tell you that you got caught up in the emotions, and you really didn't get saved. That is a lie from the enemy. You are starting to grow in your walk with God and learning the difference between hearing God's voice and hearing what the enemy tries to tell you.

A great analogy is when a baby learns to move for the first time. First that baby scoots, then crawls, then begins to walk. As a parent, we need to let our children learn those steps. It's hard not to intervene each time that little one begins to walk and starts to fall. They need to find their own balance, and figure out how to walk. Just as we are as new Christians, we have to learn to walk, and sometimes God allows us to fall, so that we can learn to get up again looking at our Father!

I found a letter the other day that encouraged me. My mother kept my drawings and things as I was growing up. In the packet I found a letter from my camp counselor. Pastor Jack Ireland wrote on July 8, 1958, and here is an excerpt from that letter "It was a thrill to see you carry your Bible and note that you spent time reading it. I also appreciated your attendance at the Morning Devotions hike." I only went to church camp once and I was 12 years old. This letter reminded me that God was keeping me and drawing me to Him at an early age with a hunger for more of Him.

God will allow us to learn our lessons the hard way sometimes so we can grow in Him but it is all because He loves us! I know the Lord will satisfy your hunger for more of Him and you will love to be in His presence, feeling His heartbeat and hearing His whisper.

CHAPTER 6
THE FEAR

The fear of God that my mom put in me was a good thing. This literal fear of God kept me from getting into trouble. However the teaching about the Holy Spirit in the Assembly of God church was new to me as I was growing up. It was a different kind of fear, more from a lack of understanding about the person of the Holy Spirit and how He works in lives and does the miracles that I was seeing.

In the 1950's I saw Billy Graham and Oral Roberts in tent meetings in Phoenix. Many people came forward and accepted Jesus' forgiveness. I watched people being healed as Oral Roberts prayed for them and it was an amazing experience. However, it was just something I watched and wondered about at 7 to 10 years of age. I have since discovered that both of them had been baptized in the Holy Spirit and were being used in the gifts of the Spirit.

The sermons on the Holy Spirit at the AG church were normally on a Wednesday night. These sermons were about our need to have the power of the Holy Spirit working in our lives by being baptized in the Holy Spirit. This was totally foreign to me and I was very cautious for some years because the only instruction we received was to "tarry" and wait for this power to come into our lives.

The main Bible translation we had back in those days was the King James Version that uses the word "tarry", just like in my New King James Version. In Luke 24:49, Jesus was telling the disciples, *"Behold, I send the Promise of My Father upon you, but tarry in the city of Jerusalem until you are endued with power from on high"*. This may be where the Pentecostals received their instruction to "tarry" to receive the gift of the Holy Spirit. In the later translations and in the Amplified Bible, which I love, the words used are "wait" "stay" and "remain".

63

Maybe some of you have heard sermons on a Sunday morning that were just "hell, fire and brimstone". All of the messages with an altar call seemed to last 30 minutes with the choir singing "All to Jesus I surrender". That put the fear of God in people for sure. The church didn't seem to be growing back then unless someone came from another church or moved into town. If someone gave a message in tongues that sure scared a visitor and none of the pastors I heard never explained what the Lord was doing in these gifts of the Spirit.

As a teenager, I was in the youth group called "Christ Ambassadors" based upon Second Corinthians 5:20. I remember after the youth service the youth leader would have kids come to the front for prayer. The rest of us were standing while the worship music played and I remember this one time at a church when the youth leader came back to talk to me. He invited me to come up to the front and be prayed for to receive this "baptism in the Holy Spirit". It was still new and kind of scary to me so I refused to go.

After moving to Clovis, California in 1971, I remember having a hunger for more of Jesus in my life and going to the altar to "tarry for the baptism". At that point I had a lot of new fears. I was so confused because one person would tell me to "hold on", and someone else told me to "let go". I had no idea how to receive this baptism in the Holy Spirit.

As the months went by I remember being at the altar crying and begging God to baptize me in the Holy Spirit. I wanted more of Jesus and this Holy Spirit in my life. Sometimes I would open my mouth and wait for God to take my tongue and make me start speaking in a heavenly language. As people were praying and crying sometimes they started to stutter and I heard someone say "you got it", referring to their "spiritual language". I never wanted someone to say "Jerry got it" because I didn't want "it". I wanted the baptism in the Holy Spirit that was supposed to give me power to live for Christ and be a better witness!

So here again, was the fear of the unknown. It was a lack of understanding as a result of an absence of teaching and instruction. I left the church disappointed, confused and fearful that I was a terrible sinner and not worthy of this experience. I thought I had to work harder at being a good Christian so I would be worthy to receive the baptism in the Holy Spirit.

Oh my, how I tried to be perfect, never sin or do anything stupid so I would be worthy to receive the gift of the Spirit. No, I never succeeded in those endeavors. I discovered that God's gift of salvation is free and so is the baptism in the Holy Spirit! We cannot "earn" either one by what we do, or how perfect we try to be.

In the letter to the church at Ephesus, Paul wrote in Ephesians 2:8 and 9, *"For by grace you have been saved through faith, and that not of yourselves; it is the gift of God, not of works, lest anyone should boast."* The same principle applies to this gift of the baptism in the Holy Spirit because we will never be so "godly" or "holy" that God will finally be able to work in our lives. He uses imperfect people to touch the world for Christ just like those 12 very imperfect disciples fed the multitude. They had to step out in faith to take their little basket of food while looking at a thousand hungry families in front of each of them. They sure weren't perfect!

One of the last fears I can remember that concerned me was about being in the grocery store or in a restaurant and uncontrollably start speaking in tongues. People would think I had lost my mind or that I was on drugs. My friend let me assure you that will never happen. You will not be "overcome" by the Spirit and start speaking in tongues and be "out of control". You will be in total control and can start and stop speaking in tongues anytime you want. This is not something that we flaunt because it is very personal and special in our walking in the Spirit and relationship with Jesus.

Having some fears and concerns is a normal thing and the enemy of our soul will feed on any fears just to keep us from having that power of the Holy Spirit in our lives to overcome him. That is why I am sharing with you the truth and the reality of this wonderful experience so you can overcome your fears. Rest assured, the Holy Spirit will not make you do anything you do not want to do.

CHAPTER 7
THE PROMISE OF THE FATHER

There are many books that cover the baptism in the Holy Spirit and do an excellent job. At the end of this book I will list some of the ones I have read that have been a blessing to me.

As I read in the Old Testament, the Spirit of God would come upon a person for a specific task, for leadership or a powerful encounter. Sometimes it was for one moment, sometimes for a longer period of time. Thank the Lord that today the Holy Spirit comes to dwell in us at the moment we accept Jesus Christ and He stays with us to help us in our walk with Christ.

For example, in the Old Testament the Spirit of God was placed on people to make clothing items and articles for the tabernacle. Sometimes, this happened when men were anointed to lead a nation like Saul and later David were anointed as king. There are different terms used for the Spirit working in the Old Testament and some of them are even used in the New Testament.

In Exodus 28, the LORD spoke to Moses and told him to make sacred garments for Aaron. In verse 3 it reads, *So you shall speak to all who are gifted artisans, whom I have filled with the spirit of wisdom, that they may make Aaron's garments...*, so in this text the LORD had "filled them with the spirit of wisdom".

Do you understand why I am typing the name LORD in capital letters? In the Old Testament when the name of the LORD is in capital letters it is also written as YHWH in Hebrew, meaning the one true Creator God. In Exodus 3:13-15, God identifies Himself to Moses as *I AM WHO I AM* and in Hebrew it means "to be" and implies the absolute existence of God.

Reading Numbers chapter 11, Moses gathered seventy men from the elders of the people. In verse 25, the LORD came down and took of the Spirit that was upon him (Moses), and placed the same upon the seventy elders; and it happened *when the Spirit rested upon them, that they prophesied...*, so here the Spirit "rested upon" them.

In Judges 3:9-10 the LORD raised up Othniel to be the deliverer for the children of Israel and the Spirit of the LORD "came upon" him and he judged Israel.

Reading 1 Samuel 10, Samuel had previously poured oil on Saul because God had anointed him Commander over His people. In verse 10, Saul met the group of prophets as Samuel had prophesied, and *the Spirit of God came upon him, and he prophesied among them.*

In 1 Samuel 16:13 Samuel took the horn of oil and anointed him (David) in the midst of his brothers. Here the *Spirit of the LORD came upon David from that day forward.*

Did you notice in the Old Testament that it states *the Spirit of the LORD* or *the Spirit of God* and not the Holy Spirit? In the New Testament Jesus talked about believers being baptized in the Holy Spirit. These are not two separate Spirits of God but when Jesus came to earth to save us from sin, He said He had to leave so the Holy Spirit would come. He said the Father promised to send us a Helper, the Holy Spirit who is also our Comforter and He will help guide us.

Ezekiel states that the Spirit *fell upon me* in Chapter 11 verse 5. So these are a few examples of the Spirit working in the Old Testament and the different terms used. You will see some of these terms used again after the baptism in the Holy Spirit in Acts 2:4. We read the prophecy by Joel of the outpouring of the Holy Spirit in Joel 2:28, *And it shall come to pass afterward that I will pour out My Spirit on all flesh.* This was fulfilled in Acts 2:4 on the Day of Pentecost. As Peter stood up to preach he quoted Joel in Acts 2:16-21.

When John the Baptist was baptizing people in water for repentance, he told them in Matthew 3:11 that ...*He who is coming after me is mightier than I, whose sandals I am not worthy to carry.* Then John said, *He will baptize you with the Holy Spirit and fire.* Some versions do not include the word *fire.* Often readers miss the part where Jesus is the baptizer in the Holy Spirit and that it is a promise from the Father.

In Mark 1:7-8 it states that John was not worthy to stoop down and loose Jesus' sandal strap. Then in verse 8, John said, *I indeed baptize you with water but He will baptize you with the Holy Spirit.* This is also shown in Luke 3:16.

Don't forget, John was baptizing people for repentance. In other words they were believing for salvation but Jesus would baptize them in the Holy Spirit later. So these people were now believers, which shows that the baptism in the Holy Spirit is a separate work of the Spirit.

Jesus had already chosen His disciples and in Matthew 10:1 ...*He had called His twelve disciples to Him, He gave them power over unclean spirits, to cast them out, and to heal all kinds of sickness and all kinds of disease.* In the Amplified Classic Version of that same scripture it reads ...*He gave them power and authority.* When we read in Luke 9:1-2 it says *Then He called His twelve disciples together and He gave them power and authority over all demons, and to cure diseases. He sent them to preach the kingdom of God and to heal the sick.*

When you are given authority that means you are under authority. I have an example of authority having been in law enforcement for most of my life. When a Police Academy Graduate is being hired with a police department they raise their right hand to uphold the laws of the land and they are given a badge and a gun. Now that officer has just as much authority and powers as the Chief of Police and represents the Chief to the public. Of course the Chief has much more experience and training than the new officer, but the officer still has as much authority and power as the Chief. Just like that officer, when we accept Christ we now have Christ's authority but we need training to handle that power in the right way, and we must represent Christ to the public.

If someone asks about the twelve disciples who were already casting out demons and healing the sick and they weren't baptized in the Holy Spirit so why do I have to be baptized in the Holy Spirit? I remind them that the disciples were given "authority" by Jesus to do the same miracles that Jesus did while they were under His authority. But when Jesus left He sent the Holy Spirit to empower them, and us, to do the work and continue ministering in the authority and power of the Holy Spirit. As we see in the book of Acts, after they were baptized in the Holy Spirit they continued to heal the sick and cast out demons, plus they now had power to become witnesses of Jesus death and resurrection. As a result, the Holy Spirit brings people to repentance and they surrender to Christ. That same power of the Holy Spirit is available to us today and we need to stay under the authority of Jesus Christ.

In John 14:16-17 Jesus said He would pray to the Father and *...He will give you another Helper, that He may abide with you forever, the Spirit of Truth, whom the world cannot receive, because it neither sees Him nor knows Him; but you know Him, for He dwells with you and will be in you.* When Jesus said *"whom the world cannot receive"* He is referring to those who are not believers in Jesus Christ.

So this "Helper", the Holy Spirit, also called the "Spirit of Truth" is only for believers. This is an interesting verse when Jesus told the disciples that you know Him (the Holy Spirit), for He dwells "with you" and He will be "in you". As you read the gospels for example the Holy Spirit went with them, spoke to them, cautioned them but He was never residing "in them". Now Jesus said that "He will be in you", knowing the Holy Spirit would enter them as we see next.

In John chapter 20, Jesus had risen from the dead that morning and in verse 19 to 22, Jesus appeared to them that evening where the disciples were hiding for fear of the Jews. Jesus first words were *Peace be with you.* I am sure they were shocked as Jesus just appeared in the room with them. In verse 21 Jesus said to them again *Peace to you! As the Father has sent Me, I also send you.* Then in verse 22 *And when he had said this, He breathed on them and said to them, Receive the Holy Spirit....* This is when the Holy Spirit first indwelt the disciples. Jesus said earlier that He (the Holy Spirit) was with them and would be "in them". When we accept Christ into our lives the Holy Spirit comes to dwell "in us" just as He breathed on the disciples.

That is when the Holy Spirit first started to dwell in the believers; of course it was the disciples at that time. When Jesus said that He must go so the Helper, the Holy Spirit would be sent is about the baptism in the Holy Spirit. This is a separate work of the Holy Spirit in a person's life after being filled with the Spirit at salvation.

Jesus could not stay with the disciples. If He had, then the work of the cross would be so limited. But He said in John 16:7 *...it is to your advantage that I go away, for if I do not go away, the Helper will not come to you, but if I depart, I will send Him to you.* The Helper, the Holy Spirit, will baptize the 120 in the upper room and they will speak in tongues.

In Luke 24:49 Jesus said, *Behold, I send the Promise of My Father upon you; but tarry in the city of Jerusalem until you are endued with power from on high.* After Jesus rose from the dead he was seen by over 500 witnesses on 12 separate occasions. One of those times was 40 days later when He appeared to the disciples in the upper room where they were hiding. When He said *not many days from now* He was referring to Pentecost that would occur 10 days from then. Pentecost refers to 50 and it would be 50 days from the resurrection to when the Holy Spirit would come down in that upper room on the Day of Pentecost and tongues of fire would rest upon each one of them.

In Acts 1:4-6, Luke is reminding the disciples that when Jesus was with them that He commanded them to wait. The scripture reads *And being assembled together with them, He commanded them not to depart from Jerusalem, but to wait for the Promise of the Father, which, He said, You have heard from Me, for John truly baptized with water, but you shall be baptized with the Holy Spirit not many days from now.* Notice the word "commanded" does not mean "suggested".

When Jesus told them to wait for the promise of the Father, He was speaking truth because Jesus is the Truth. He knew more than the disciples did at that time how much they would need the power of the Holy Spirit in their lives by being baptized in the Holy Spirit. This is the same reason for us to have power in our lives today to tell the world about God's love and salvation, not just to speak in tongues.

Speaking in tongues is just part of the package of the baptism in the Holy Spirit. Speaking in tongues builds us up in the Spirit according to 1 Corinthians 14:4 and Jude verses 20-21. I cannot explain it, I trust that the Bible is God's word and I know that the Holy Spirit does a work in me when I pray in the Spirit using my spiritual language. I also believe the Holy Spirit knows what my day holds and when I pray in my spiritual language that He helps to prepare me for what comes my way.

Look what else happened when the Holy Spirit came and baptized them. As we read in John 14:25-26 where Jesus was speaking to the disciples *These things I have spoken to you while being present with you. But the Helper, the Holy Spirit, whom the Father will send in My name, He will teach you all things, and bring to your remembrance all things that I said to you.* Of course, after the disciples were baptized in the Holy Spirit they started to remember the things that Jesus had said and the Holy Spirit started teaching them and using them in a powerful way as we read through the book of Acts.

In Acts 1:5, Luke was reminding the disciples that Jesus told them that they would be baptized with the Holy Spirit *not many days from now*. In verse 8, Luke reminded them that Jesus said that they would be witnesses in Jerusalem, Judea, and Samaria and to the uttermost parts of the world. That is the purpose of the baptism in the Holy Spirit is to evangelize the world. For example, when God uses people to pray for someone and they are healed, that brings glory to God and lets that person know that God is real. Then that person may come into a relationship with Jesus which is a result of evangelism in action, touching the world for Christ including the gift of healing being used to bring God glory.

Let me interject a story here. I was deer hunting in North Carolina with my nephew in 2009. He took me to his friend's farm to hunt and I was able to harvest a buck. In March, I called Kirk and thanked him for allowing me to hunt on his farm. He told me that he had a torn retina, which I know is very critical. I asked him if he was lying down and being still. Kirk said, "No, I have the farm, the butcher shop and my concrete business going so I don't have time to lie down". I asked Kirk if I could pray for him on the phone and he hesitated what seemed to be 5 minutes, then said, "Oh, okay". So I prayed for God to touch his eye and bring healing because I know God is the healer. I did not feel any heat, or any emotions or anything else when I prayed!

I called Kirk in May to check on him. He said, "Jerry do you remember when you prayed for me a couple months ago? I was having such severe headaches from the torn retina that I had to pull my car off the road. I couldn't work or work on the computer. I have not had a headache since you prayed for me". My friend, that is not about my "holiness", I am just an imperfect vessel in the hands of the Holy Spirit that He can work through when He wants to. Healing is one of the 9 gifts of the Holy Spirit in 1 Corinthians 12.

To make a long story short, Kirk took his wife and two boys, about 6 and 8, to church the next Sunday and they all accepted Jesus Christ in their lives. Kirk told me he bought 4 of the same Bibles for each of his family members. Since then, I have hunted there and went to church with them. That is a perfect example of "evangelism". He was sick, I prayed, God healed Kirk and revealed Himself to the family and they all believed in Jesus. So the Lord used healing to bring a whole family to salvation. Now that is what I am talking about! This is all for God's glory and not for mine.

In the New Spirit Filled Life Bible, reading Matthew 21:25 Jesus asked the Chief Priest and elders about the baptism of John, if it was it from heaven or from men. The word baptism used here is explained in my Bible in a Word Wealth commentary. Baptism is from the original Greek word *baptisma*. It is from the word *baptizo*, to dip, or immerse. *Baptisma* emphasizes the result of the act rather than the act itself of being put under the water in baptism.

In Christian water baptism the stress is on the baptized person's identification with Christ in death, burial and resurrection. So in water baptism a person is now identified with Christ and enters into the Christian community of believers.

In the baptism in the Holy Spirit experience, a person is empowered by the Holy Spirit which emphasizes the result of the baptism as it reads in Acts 1:8 so that we will receive power to become witnesses for Christ. Now we step out in boldness and in love.

As we read in Acts 1, there were 120 people in that upper room and these included Jesus mother and other women. Interesting how in the beginning his brothers did not believe their "big brother" was sent from God and would tease him and make fun of Him, read John 7:1-5. Now His brothers were in the upper room because they knew Jesus had come down to earth from heaven and there was no joking anymore! This promise of the Father is for men, women and children too, anyone who hungers and thirsts for more of Jesus! They were all together and expecting what Jesus promised.

The promise of the Father came on Pentecost and they were all in one accord. That means in unity, in agreement, waiting for what Jesus had told them. I can see them now sitting in chairs, on the floor, walking around the room worshipping, praying and just wondering what it was going to be like to be baptized in the Holy Spirit.

Now in Acts 2:3-4 it reads that there were tongues as of fire that came down and sat upon each one of them. Some people do feel heat when the Spirit comes upon them. I did not feel any heat or any other sensation when I was baptized in the Holy Spirit. They were all filled with the Holy Spirit and began to speak with other tongues as the Spirit gave the utterance. I think "all" means all 120 of them so no one was left out of this outpouring of the Holy Spirit on that Pentecost Day!

See what happens when there is a hunger and thirst for more of Jesus? In Matthew 5 Jesus is sharing about the Beatitudes and in verse 6 He said, *Blessed are those who hunger and thirst for righteousness, for they shall be filled.* All 120 were expecting, hungry and they were filled with the Spirit (indwelt).

I want to jump in here and share some visual aids with you that I have used for years in my teaching at Men's Retreats and with others. This will lead up to what I believe might make it easier to understand the difference of being "filled with the Spirit" and being "baptized in the Holy Spirit". As my friend Robert shared with me when he saw me demonstrate this to him, he said, "that is a very simple illustration of a very powerful work of the Spirit". The Lord needs to make things simple for me to understand.

As you can see in the drawings of the two glasses below, the first glass on the left represents a person who is a "big sinner" (yes I know there are not classes of sinners but just bear with me). They have done all kinds of things like stealing, hurting people, lying and cheating and so on.

The drawing of the glass on the right is that same person. When I push the trash down inside the glass below the rim I say, "Even if they try to hide their sin everyone can see it and everyone knows they are still a sinner".

This next drawing of a glass represents a person who has "just a little sin in their life", but we know that is not possible, because sin is sin in God's eyes. But for the sake of showing the difference between these two types of people I use a glass with just a little bit of trash in the bottom.

The third glass above shows how this person is honest, a good dependable worker, and a great neighbor. They love their spouse and kids. They are kind, generous and you could not find too many people as awesome as this person. The only problem is that they are still a sinner. They have not repented, asked Jesus for forgiveness for their sins and submitted to His Lordship.

The next glass below looks clear as a bell. People looking at this person may think they are really "Religious" and they are right. This was more like me; I was more religious than anything. This was me growing up like a Pharisee, a white washed wall on the outside, judgmental and critical of others on the inside. I was raised in legalism, and religion is bondage but I did not know the love and freedom that Jesus brings.

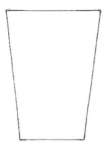

Even though the glass looks clear and "pure" I will now reveal what I was really like. I folded up a piece of paper and marked it "**PRIDE**" in bold letters. Then I rolled it up with the letters inside so you only see the white from the outside and I placed it inside the glass. As I am teaching about this prideful person, I pull the paper out of the glass, unrolled it and turned it to show the group with the word **PRIDE** showing.

Remember that we are all equal at the foot of the cross. I tell them that when we ask Jesus to forgive our sins that He comes into our life and washes away all of our sin by His shed blood on the cross. Then I picked up the glass and started acting as though I was washing the glass. Jesus cleanses us completely and now we are "Just-if-id" as though we had never sinned.

At that point I hold up the glass and tell them that this is a clean vessel that the Lord can fill, use and flow through. I use a pitcher of water since the Holy Spirit is also referred to as water in John 7:37-39. As shown in the drawing below the Holy Spirit is being poured out into the earthen clay vessel that has been cleansed from sin, Acts 10:44-45.

I think of Romans 5:5 where it says *Now hope does not disappoint, because the love of God has been poured out in our hearts by the Holy Spirit who was given to us"*. Remember that God is love! Don't forget the earlier scripture that said the Holy Spirit would be "poured out".

When I finish filling the glass I try to get the water to come to the very top of the brim or if I can make it to go over the top of the brim without spilling. Have you ever tried filling a glass with water over the brim without it spilling over? I think most everyone has tried that as a kid. Well, just think of it this way, when you come to Christ and He forgives you of all your sin, then He fills you over the brim with the Spirit. You cannot be filled up any more with the Spirit; you are full to the max. That is why every believer is actually "SPIRT FILLED" no matter if your Baptist, Lutheran or Assembly of God. If you have repented and asked Jesus Christ to forgive you of your sins, you have become a child of God and been adopted into the family of God.

The scripture tells us that the Spirit Himself bears witness with our spirit that we are children of God in Romans 8:16. I suggest you also read verses 15 to 17. Remember I told you that the spirit of man is always in lower case but the Holy Spirit is always capitalized? As you read the Word you will continue to see that in the Scripture.

One of the problems in our communication is that "us Pentecostals" or "Charismatics" have used the term "we are Spirit Filled" referring to the baptism of the Holy Spirit. Or we attend a "Spirit Filled church" referring to a church that believes in the baptism of the Holy Spirit and speaking in tongues, as well as the gifts of the Spirit.

Well dear friend, if you are born again of the Spirit, then you are "spirit filled". This is actually a very humbling experience that God would fill each of us broken clay vessels with Himself, so that He can flow through us to love and minister to others in this world. He is doing this even while He is still working on us to make us more Christ-like.

It is so sad that there are some people who have been baptized in the Holy Spirit and act as though they are holier than others. They may even put others down or tell them they are not complete in Jesus. My friend, this is not a badge to wear, this experience just draws me closer to the Lord and makes me better than I was before, to quote Pastor Bill Chaney. I love what Pastor John Amstutz said about being baptized in the Holy Spirit, "I do not get more of the Holy Spirit but the Holy Spirit gets more of me"! That is exactly what it is all about, more of Jesus in me!

I hope you see that every believer who is born again is really "Spirit filled". We grow in the Lord by being in the Word of God, in prayer, fellowship and desiring to know Him more. When we start hungering and thirsting for more of Jesus, a time comes when our soul longs for more of the Lord. Our lives are so thirsty for more of Him that we become desperate for Him and He responds to that kind of heart!

Next I take this clean glass that represents a "spirit filled" person and drop it into the pitcher of water (the Holy Spirit). That person is now "baptized" or immersed in the Holy Spirit as shown below in my drawing.

This is a simple illustration describing the difference of being filled with the Spirit at conversion and actually being "baptized in the Holy Spirit". You may hear others say "baptized by the Holy Spirit" or "baptized with the Holy Spirit". All of these terms mean the same thing.

If you take an empty glass and drop it into the pitcher it will not go under the water. So if a person is not born again of the Spirit, or saved, they cannot be baptized in the Holy Spirit.

When I take the glass out of the pitcher of water, which represents the Holy Spirit, it is dripping water everywhere. I then take the glass and bring it across the top of the other two glasses that represent people who are not born again. The joy of the Lord that is in you can't help but drip love and joy on others as the Holy Spirit has done in you. When they see your life and feel Jesus Love as you share Jesus with them, you are an example of Jesus Christ. When I say share with a person I don't mean "preach at them", they will know you are different. I am saying just be kind and loving to them bearing the fruit of the Spirit shown in Galatians 5:22-23.

You can share things that Jesus has done for you or how He answered your prayers. This does not put them on the defense so they can listen to you and they can accept it or reject it. The Holy Spirit does the work and it is not our job to convert anyone.

I sold a dirt bike to a person from out of town and we became friends riding in the Sierra Mountains. I never preached at him, I just shared things that the Lord was doing my life and answers to prayer. I just kept loving him and one day he said my life reflected what a real Christian is supposed to be.

Several years later he called me and said that he had accepted Jesus Christ into his life. He and his wife are serving the Lord, including his son with his family all in Visalia. Let your light shine before men so God gets the glory. In Matthew 5:14-16 It reads *You are the light of the world...In the same way, let your light shine before others, that they may see your good deeds and glorify your Father in heaven.*

In Matthew 22:36-40 the attorney asked Jesus what is the greatest commandment and Jesus told him *You shall love the LORD your God with all your heart, with all your soul, and with all your mind. This is the first and great commandment. And the second is like it, you shall love your neighbor as yourself.* Then Jesus made a profound statement, *On these two commandments hang all the Law and Prophets.*

In John 13:34 Jesus made an interesting statement, *A new commandment I give you: Love one another. As I have loved you, so you must love one another. By this everyone will know that you are my disciples, if you love one another.*

Our faith in Jesus Christ presents us faultless before the Father, pure, righteous and profoundly justified. Then our experience of being baptized into Christ at the time of our salvation and our experience of water baptism, as well as our experience of the baptism in the Holy Spirit should only draw us into a deeper and more intimate relationship with Jesus. This will result in the Holy Spirit accomplishing His work in and through our lives to touch the world for eternity.

Be on guard that you do not live on the feelings or emotions of any of those experiences, no matter how awesome they were at the time. Feelings and emotions can fade so we must live and walk by faith according to the word of God. When you don't feel that warmth or "holy ghost goose bumps" you do what you know to do anyway.

Those original emotions or feelings are gone but I know that Jesus bore the stripes for our healing, so I pray for a person for healing even though I don't feel a thing. The results are up to the Lord. When that person is healed I can't take the credit and if that person is not healed I don't have to take the blame. At times Jesus healed "all" of the sick. Sometimes He only healed one, like the blind man. So I just try to be obedient when I feel the Holy Spirit prompting me to pray for someone or when the Spirit gives me a word to share something with someone.

There have been times when I felt prompted to speak to someone or pray for them and I walked away or said good-bye as I walked out the door. You will know when you failed to obey. I knew right away that I grieved the Holy Spirit and if possible I call that person back or do what I knew to do if I can. My heart aches when I fail to obey, I'm still in the process of maturing. When you have experienced a touch from heaven and start maturing in your walk with the Lord you won't need those "feelings" to encourage you as you continue your walk of faith with Christ.

In saying that we are Spirit filled at conversion, this also implies that the Spirit comes to dwell in us. In Webster's Dictionary, the word "dwell" is defined as "to live as a resident". This means that if you dwell in your home then you have access to the entire house. You live there as the resident and the enemy is not welcome. When you are baptized in the Holy Spirit, you now give Him access to your entire home, including your secret locked closet.

Remember, "love is the key"! The baptism in the Holy Spirit is a baptism of love and power so your life will be a river of love flowing out of you. The Holy Spirit will use you to bring others into this river of life in Jesus, who is the baptizer in the Holy Spirit as promised by the heavenly Father.

CHAPTER 8
THE EXPERIENCE

It is amazing how the Holy Spirit continues to enlighten me and teach me even as I am writing this book. I sure don't know it all. In my devotional this morning with Oswald Chambers reading June 13, I like what he said in essence, "I am not trying to make my experience a principal for you, but I hope you will allow God to be as creative and original to you as He was with me". The Lord knows you and He will work in you in His own special way. That way you will know without a doubt that God has done something in you.

So I just ask that you continue to read my story and do not feel that I am pressuring you or trying to argue with you if you do not believe in the baptism in the Holy Spirit. Maybe you believe that it was only for the days of the apostles. I just want to share my story with you and what I have experienced for 47 years of my life.

As I have previously mentioned, I struggled with this teaching and was hesitant to let anyone lay hands on me or pray for me. I guess I acted as though this experience others had was like the plague, "Don't come near me!" That is until I started having a greater desire to be baptized in the Holy Spirit after I moved to California, in November of 1971. I still didn't understand it but I had such a hunger for more of Jesus in my life and I would beg God and cry, "Oh God, baptize me in the Holy Spirit". I probably did a lot of confessing before I knelt to pray because I had not been perfect. I knew I had to be a better Christian to "deserve" this gift of the Holy Spirit. Oh how wrong I was back then but I didn't understand this was a free gift just as salvation is a free gift.

In February, 1973, we had a visiting evangelist, Claude O. Wood, who came to our church. I found out later that he was originally from the church I was attending. He was traveling around the world and leading people into the baptism of the Holy Spirit, including Catholics and people from other denominations. I have no clue what he preached on that Sunday night. But at the end of the service he said, "If anyone wants to be baptized in the Holy Spirit come down to the front". I was there in 2 seconds and then he invited us to come to the back room so we did. We stood in a circle and he told us to start worshipping and praising the Lord. We didn't kneel down and he never prayed for us or laid hands on us. I started speaking words of praise and thankfulness to the Lord and other people were raising their hands and worshipping.

Well, since I wanted to be baptized in the Holy Spirit and receive my "spiritual language" I stopped praising the Lord and stood there with my mouth open and hands raised to heaven. I have always expected the Lord to take my tongue and start speaking through me in a spiritual language, but nothing happened. Two words came to my mind that I did not understand and they sounded funny or weird. I sure wasn't going to say those two words. I must have made them up! I could have heard someone else using those two words and I was just repeating what I may have heard them say.

The following Wednesday night I was back at the altar and begging and crying to have Jesus baptize me in the Holy Spirit. A lady came down and knelt next to me and prayed with me. When I was done and still sniffling, she looked at me and said, "Jerry, normally the Holy Spirit will give you the words to speak and then you have to speak them out". Oh really? I will have to think about that.

The next Sunday night to my surprise, here came Claude O. Wood to speak again. Wow this is great; I wonder if he will pray for people to receive the baptism in the Holy Spirit. I don't know what he preached on but guess what? He invited us down to the front if we wanted to be baptized in the Holy Spirit and then he invited us into the back room.

There we were, standing in a circle again and all he wanted us to do was worship and praise the Lord. As we all stood with our hands raised and worshipping the Lord all of a sudden those two words came to my mind again from last Sunday. Okay, so if the Holy Spirit brings the words to my mind, then I have to speak them out. At least that is what I was told.

I decided that I was not going to say them too loud because I didn't want anyone hearing me and saying "Oh Jerry you got baptized in the Holy Spirit". So I started saying my two "strange" words real quietly. The only problem was that each time I took a breath and breathed in I spoke the words out a little louder. With every breath I breathed in it was like I had a balloon inside and it would pump up bigger. With every breath my chest and insides kept feeling like I was getting blown up and my words kept getting louder and louder as I spoke them!

Remember that God breathed into man the breath of life? Jesus breathed on the disciples and said, "Receive the Holy Spirit". The Holy Spirit is referred to as breath and every time I took a breath the Holy Spirit was breathing into me and I breathed out praise in a new language! As I continued to speak my two words out loud I felt like I was getting "filled up inside". I started weeping with joy as I felt the love and presence of Jesus. It wasn't long and I was crying for joy and speaking my two words louder and louder as I worshipped the Lord standing in His presence. Now I am thinking that Romans 5:5 is about me as it says the Love of God was poured out into **my** heart and life by the Holy Spirit. This verse may not just be for salvation but for the baptism in the Holy Spirit also!

Oh my, February 11, 1973 was a wonderful night! The only way I can describe what happened to me is that I was baptized in love. Remember God is love, 1 John 4:18 *There is no fear in love; but perfect love casts out fear.* Tell me who is perfect? Who is love? So all of my fears, questions and anxiety was gone.

In the book of Acts the apostles laid hands on people and they received the baptism in the Holy Spirit. I did not have hands laid on me that night with Pastor Wood, we just stood and worshipped the Lord. In the upper room no one laid hands on them so I believe there are times people can be baptized in the Holy Spirit without the "laying on of hands".

I think of my friend Henry Miramontes who got saved at a Morris Cerullo meeting and went to a church that was going to baptize the new believers in the river. Henry came up out of the water speaking in tongues. No one actually laid hands on him to be baptized in the Holy Spirit; they just baptized him in water. He did not know what happened to him so he had to ask the people and they told him he had been baptized in the Holy Spirit and that was his personal prayer and praise language. He wasn't speaking English or Spanish when he came up out of the water! Yes, it is special when someone lays hands on a person and they receive the baptism in the Holy Spirit and release their spiritual language. But let's not put God in a box!

There are those who have been at home alone and have been hungering for the baptism in the Holy Spirit and they get baptized and release their spiritual prayer and praise language. Some have even received their prayer language in the shower or during their quiet time with the Lord. So if you are ready for the Lord to baptize you in the Holy Spirit, just ask Him and then start thanking Him! Whether you are home alone, on the phone with someone praying for you, or having someone lay hands on you, speak the words out by faith that the Holy Spirit gives you. In Acts 2:4 it says *And they were all filled with the Holy Spirit and began to speak with other tongues, **as the Spirit gave them utterance*** (emphasis added). The Holy Spirit will give you the syllable, word or words to speak.

On Monday morning on my way to work I used my two words all the way to work. However, a problem came up. While I was driving the enemy planted some thoughts in my mind and I heard the words "You just made those up, you were all emotional last night". I already learned that you need to talk to the devil and tell him a thing or two. So I said out loud, in fact with a very loud voice in my car, "Devil you're a liar, I was baptized in the Holy Spirit last night!" Then I proceeded to speak those two words in my spiritual prayer and praise language all the way to work in a loud voice in the car. That shut the devil up!

Monday night I called Barbara's parents, her sister and our brother-in-law in Phoenix and told them that I had been baptized in the Holy Spirit. Of course they all rejoiced with me and were so happy.

On Tuesday I praised the Lord all the way to work in a loud voice and the devil knew not to try anything. Tuesday evening I called my parents and brothers in Arizona and told them what happened. They also rejoiced with me. It is interesting that all three of us brothers had to move to California to get baptized in the Holy Spirit. Can anything good come from California? Yes!

On Wednesday morning, I worshipped in my two words all the way to work again. I had an assurance come to me and I knew without a doubt that I had been baptized in the Holy Spirit. It reminded me that when a person comes to Christ they must "confess" and share it out loud with others also. When we speak something our words have power and our tongue is a creative force. There is an assurance and confidence that comes when we openly confess what the Lord is doing in our lives. We become a witness in that matter or experience.

Just like confession for salvation, in Romans 10:9-10 *that if you confess with your mouth the Lord Jesus and believe in your heart that God has raised Him from the dead, you will be saved. For with the heart one believes unto righteousness, and with the mouth confession is made unto salvation.* When you tell others that you accepted Jesus Christ into your life or tell them you were baptized in the Holy Spirit, that confession is powerful and it even strengthens you.

The devil will lie, scheme, deceive and trick us any time or chance he can. In John 8:44 Jesus is speaking about the devil and said *He was a murderer from the beginning, and does not stand in the truth, because there is no truth in him. When he speaks a lie, he speaks from his own resources, for he is a liar and the father of it.* So I learned a long time ago, you need to talk to the devil and he will hear you when you speak in the authority of Jesus Christ telling him to go to Jesus and be judged by Jesus then go where Jesus tells him to go. The enemy will whisper lies and bring doubt to us. Watchman Nee, in one of his books talked about "The Battle of the Mind". So I repeat Philippians 2:5 says, *Let this mind be in you which was also in Christ Jesus.* You can win the battle if any lies or wrong thoughts come to you that are not of the Spirit.

We have the power and authority to stop any thoughts that are contrary to the Word of God and try to discourage us or tell us that we are not saved, we aren't worthy to call ourselves a Christian or we haven't been baptized in the Holy Spirit. In 2 Corinthians 10:3-5 *For though we walk in the flesh, we do not war according to the flesh. For the weapons of our warfare are not carnal but mighty in God for pulling down strongholds, casting down arguments and every high thing that exalts itself against the knowledge of God, **bringing every thought into captivity to the obedience of Christ*** (emphasis added). You have the power and choice to change thoughts.

The Holy Spirit can bring thoughts to our mind because we can have the mind of Christ and allow the Holy Spirit to speak to us. He can influence our thinking and lead us as He is our Helper and guide. When the devil tries to bring thoughts to our mind we can know the difference as to who is speaking if we are staying in intimate relationship with Jesus. I cannot stress enough the importance of being in the Word and memorizing it. Read Matthew 4 where Jesus quoted the Word and defeated the enemy in the wilderness! In Luke 4 we read the same story and also see in verse 14 *then Jesus returned in the power of the Spirit...* after he had been tempted by the devil but

90

He overcame him by the power of the written Word that Jesus quoted.

So when the devil told me I made those words up and I was just being emotional. I knew that was not the Holy Spirit speaking to me. The enemy was trying to plant those thoughts in my mind to prevent me from walking in the power of the Spirit and having authority over him.

If you are walking with Jesus do you remember the time when Jesus became alive in you. It was like you walked through a new door and things were different. My cousin Byron said that he got saved at a Billy Graham crusade but he never felt anything different. However, that next morning he stepped out the door to go to work and he never saw the sky so blue and the grass so green. It was shocking to him and he knew something happened to him in the Spirit. The baptism in the Holy Spirit experience is like walking through another door. Now His presence was so real to me but before this time I was living for Jesus on my own will power.

Meanwhile I used my two words and began falling in love deeper and deeper with Jesus, the lover of my soul (my mind, my will and my emotions) and my inner spiritual being. Like I said before, the only way I can describe what I experienced is that I was baptized in love. I fell in love with Jesus, I fell in love with the Word and I had a boldness to witness in love rather than beating people with Bible scriptures!

If I told someone, "If you don't repent and give your life to Jesus you are going to hell" that is truth. However, that is not the Spirit of Truth. The Spirit reaches out in love and draws people to the Father, convicting them of sin. The Lord is *not willing that any should perish but that all should come to repentance*, 2 Peter 3:9.

I continued to use my two words and then two weeks later we were in church worshipping in our spiritual language. All of a sudden as I was worshipping with my two words it was kind of like my tongue just started forming new words without me thinking or focusing on how to say the new words. I knew I needed to speak the new words out. As I did, more new words kept forming as I spoke in tongues and I had a whole new sentence. What joy!

That experience was the only time my spiritual prayer and praise language increased like that at a specific time. Many times people start out speaking a syllable, or a word, and their language grows as they exercise their new spiritual language. Some people get a whole paragraph and some seem to get a whole language. In a way it is like a baby learning to talk.

Since that time that I got a whole sentence from just two words, my language has grown without me realizing it. I just know that when I have been interceding for someone or just in deep worship loving Jesus that my language changes. I have one specific language that I speak all the time when I am worshipping or praying. There are times that my language changes again when I am coming against the evil one. My language changes with a force and I start praying in an authoritative voice with power knowing that the Holy Spirit knows what I need to pray against the enemy who is trying to destroy someone's life or wreak havoc in a marriage.

Often when I am singing some simple worship choruses with my guitar during my special time alone with the Lord, I start singing in the spirit while I am strumming chords. My voice changes the melody with the chords. I can't sing or keep a beat but Jesus loves to hear me sing to Him!

Pastor John Amstutz was teaching on the baptism in the Holy Spirit some years ago and was throwing out small candy bars to the congregation to emphasize that this was a "free gift" just like the candy bars were a free gift. Well, the Lord started expanding this is in my mind.

In my teaching I adopted this concept and purchased different "fun size" candy bars and gift wrapped them in a variety of different paper. In my classes at Central Valley Teen Challenge I made one for every student. First I asked them if they would like a free gift. I explained that they had no idea what the gift was, but that they would love it. Of course they wanted one, so I told them not to open it until I tell them. I told them they had to ask me for it, so they would say, "Jerry, may I have this free gift?" Then I handed it to them with great joy, just like the Father does when we ask Him for this free gift of the baptism in the Holy Spirit that the Father promised.

Then I asked them "Do you see that the others have the free gift also but it looks different?" I tell them that Jesus will give you this gift and it may happen totally different for you than someone else. Then I asked them if they had the faith to open their free gift but don't eat it yet. As they are unwrapping the candy I explained to them that theirs was different than the others because God can give His gift in different ways. It will be very special just for you.

Next I explained to them that in order to "receive" the joy of this gift you must "open your mouth" so you can praise Him in the Spirit. Finally I told them, "Okay men, open your mouth and enjoy your free gift". It is the same when you are baptized in the Holy Spirit, you must open your mouth as the Holy Spirit gives you the words to speak. You need to speak them out loud. Remember that you may only get one or two syllables or a couple words or maybe a whole sentence comes to your mind. You speak them out by faith.

As you speak them out loud, you hear yourself saying the words. What does the scripture say in Romans 10:17? *So then faith comes by hearing, and hearing by the word of God.* Yes that is talking about the Word of God that people hear and then have the faith to come to Christ. Could it also mean when you hear the words of the Spirit that you are speaking out loud that possibly this builds your faith also and encourages you? When you hear yourself speaking in tongues it also gives you a confirmation in your spirit that "I have been baptized in the Holy Spirit"!

When you have a hunger for more of the Lord in your life and you want to make Jesus Christ Lord in every area of your life, then you will desire to have everything the Lord has to offer you. Have an open heart and an open mouth. The Holy Spirit wants to speak to you and direct your steps in new ways! Get ready for an exciting journey!

CHAPTER 9
THE TESTIMONIES

For decades I have interviewed many people asking them specifically how did they release their spiritual prayer and praise language. Through my years of teaching and learning I have seen how the Lord normally works in a person's life baptizing them in the Holy Spirit and giving them the words to speak. As I have said before, a person has to have the faith to receive and to speak the words out, because the words do not make sense and they may sound weird or like a baby to us. Remember, since it is a spiritual language and may sound very strange we can have a fear of speaking the words out loud, that is where faith comes in again, like for salvation.

If you come from a background where you do not pray out loud then you will have to start worshipping the Lord out loud in your prayer time and praise Him when you are at home, in your car, or in the shower. Remember in Acts 2:4 it said, *They began to speak.* The Lord will not take your tongue and start making sounds like I expected Him to do. You will have to speak the words out as they come to you in your mind. Words also may just start flowing out of your innermost being without you even thinking about any words. Just start speaking them out.

So here are some examples of how God has worked in some lives. Remember, you cannot put the God in a box! He wants to give you this gift in a way that will be special just for you.

When my wife was about 5 or 6 years old she had a hunger for more of Jesus. Her dad told me that after church one evening she went to the altar and knelt there. When he went to get her so they could drive home he heard her speaking in her spiritual language. He picked her up from kneeling at the altar "speaking in tongues" and carried her to the car "speaking in tongues", then drove all the way home to Scottsdale for 30 minutes "speaking in tongues", then carried her in the house and put her in bed "speaking in tongues". That is the work of the Holy Spirit, she did not make up those words and she definitely was not under the influence of the devil.

Here is another story of a young tender open heart who loved Jesus at an early age. In 1976, we were at a conference and during the worship service at West Coast Bible College, my son Luke was standing next to me. While we were worshipping I turned to look at Luke and he wasn't there. He was kneeling at his chair so I knelt down next to him to pray for him and I heard him speaking in his own spiritual language at about age 7 or 8. That shows that Jesus will respond to a hungry heart for more of Him even when a person has not read any books or been instructed in any way about this experience. It is a hungry heart and the simple faith of a small child. How amazing!

Luke's wife Kathy told me that she was 4 years old when she asked Jesus to come into her life. She heard about the baptism in the Holy Spirit and really desired to have this experience. Here is what she shared with me. "I distinctly remember hearing about the baptism in the Holy Spirit and asking my mom to pray with me for that too because I wanted that. It was weeks or months after inviting Jesus into my heart. I was never told about a spiritual language that I can remember. I was just hanging out on the swing set and I was singing... which I believe is why my mom was so surprised!"

Kathy's mother went into the back yard and saw Kathy on the swing. She heard Kathy singing in the spirit as she was swinging back and forth. I can see Kathy now. She has had such a hunger in her heart for more of the Lord all these years!

I also know others who were "saved" at a very early age and were also baptized in the Holy Spirit when they are young. Children have such an open heart for the Lord when they are raised in a Christian home. The Bible says that we are to come to the Lord as little children even if we are an adult.

On a Friday years ago I met Michael for lunch one day and he was sharing with me about his desire for the baptism in the Holy Spirit. I explained the work of the Spirit to him and when we walked out of the pizza parlor, we stood on the sidewalk talking some more. I told him, "I am going to lay my hand on your shoulder but you do not have to close your eyes, and I will pray for you to be baptized in the Holy Spirit". When I finished praying, I told him that he could release his spiritual language driving back to work in the car. Then I said, "Call me and let me know". I was shocked when I said that. Well he never called me that afternoon or Saturday.

Here is an example of laying a hand on the person's shoulder right in front of a pizza parlor and praying for a person. I did not have Michael "ask the Father" for the promise to be baptized in the Holy Spirit. It is amazing how God can work through us even if we don't "do it right" or even when a new believer doesn't know one scripture verse but they can witness to someone and lead them to Jesus!

On Sunday morning I was sitting in church and before the service started and I got a tap on the shoulder. I turned around and there was my friend Michael, grinning from ear to ear. He said, "Jerry it was just like you said, I released my spiritual language in the car driving back to work Friday". Thank you Jesus. That had to be the Spirit speaking through me when I told him he could release his language in the car and to call me Friday to let me know.

We were at a Men's Retreat at Hume Lake Christian Camp about 30 years ago and I was teaching a breakout class on the baptism in the Holy Spirit. I used a panel discussion to answer questions about the work of the Holy Spirit and to respond to those "weird questions" like, "Will I start blurting out in tongues in front of the cashier" or "will I start rolling on the floor". I believe that it helped the men to understand that the Holy Spirit will not make them do weird things like that. After I closed in prayer the men started coming forward to be prayed for without me even asking them. It was totally a work of the Holy Spirit because I did not get to close like I planned it and I lost control of the meeting. The men just came forward.

It is so awesome how God puts people together! My friend Paul Warkentine got to pray for a man sitting next to him to receive the baptism in the Holy Spirit. Paul shared with me that the man sitting next to him was from the Mennonite church so Paul understood his upbringing. Paul had also attended the Mennonite church growing up and had been baptized in the Holy Spirit. This was one of those Divine Appointments how God connects people.

George came up to be prayed for at the end of the service. Another brother and I prayed for him and we started worshipping in our spiritual language. George started speaking in his spiritual language as he heard us worshipping and praising the Lord in our language. He is now being used by God mightily in a local ministry. Something happens in our lives when we get baptized in the Holy Spirit. It's like we get ignited on fire and have a burning desire to love others and minister to them as the Spirit leads us.

A friend of mine attended one of my breakout classes at a men's retreat. He came up to me the following year and said, "Jerry, I attended your class on the baptism in the Holy Spirit last November but I didn't release my language at that time. I was recently attending a wedding rehearsal in San Luis Obispo at a Catholic Mission. As I was watching the wedding rehearsal I looked around at all the statues and I asked myself, "How can God even be in here". Jerry, when I said that I felt the Holy Spirit come over me and I released my spiritual language right there in that Catholic Mission". I am sure he spoke in his new spiritual language under his breath at the wedding rehearsal but I forgot to ask him.

By the way, you can pray in the Spirit under your breath or just in your mind. When I am witnessing to someone or sharing about the Lord, I can pray in the Spirit when they are asking me questions. I ask the Holy Spirit for wisdom in how to answer them. Remember that God is no respecter of persons, places or things. He can move and speak anywhere and anytime! You do not have to be in church, a prayer meeting or on your knees to communicate with the Lord.

I was doing investigations in the Portland area about 1974, and went to visit my cousin Syl and Roger. This was not long after I had been baptized in the Holy Spirit and I shared with them my experience. They told me that they had a desire to be baptized in the Holy Spirit for a long time and even had people come over and lay hands on them and pray for them, however, they have never released their spiritual language. Syl told me, "Jerry, one day I was driving to work and I asked the Lord if He had baptized me in the Holy Spirit as I had asked Him to do, even though I did not speak in tongues. Jerry, I had such a peace and joy come over me that I knew I had been baptized in the Holy Spirit. I had such an inner peace". I told Syl that I didn't understand it but I believed her. In my spirit I just felt a confirmation that Syl had been baptized in the Holy Spirit even though she had never spoken in tongues. That was strange to me because at that time I believed you had to speak in tongues to be baptized in the Holy Spirit.

Pastor Tim Howard made a very interesting statement some years later in the 1980s that helped me to understand what happened to Syl. He said that if a person asked him if they had to speak in tongues to be baptized in the Holy Spirit, he would say "no". However he would also tell them, that they probably will one day. If a person told him that they don't have to speak in tongues Pastor Tim would remind them of Acts 2:4 and other scriptures where speaking in tongues is a part of the baptism of the Holy Spirit".

The next year I was back in Oregon conducting investigations and I called Syl from the airport. Syl asked me to come over for dinner and that she and her husband had something to share with me. I immediately knew what it was in my spirit. At dinner that evening they shared how they had both released their spiritual language. Sometimes it may take time, so just keep loving Jesus and worshipping Him. If you have asked the Lord to baptize you in the Holy Spirit when you were alone or you had someone pray for you and possibly they laid hands on you then start thanking the Lord for the baptism in the Holy Spirit. If you have not released your spiritual language yet, do not be discouraged. Don't let the enemy tell you that you are not worthy. Take those thoughts captive according to the word of God. Keep worshipping the Lord and telling Him you love Him. One day you won't have the words to tell Him you love Him in your own earthly language.

My oldest brother Ralph shared with me that he had been seeking more of Jesus and wanted to be baptized in the Holy Spirit. He said, "Jerry, I was just kneeling there at the altar one evening after the service and trying to tell Jesus how much I loved Him. It seemed I just ran out of words and I looked up and I saw Jesus standing up on the platform and my spiritual language just started flowing out of me as I worshipped Him". That is so awesome!

I had one man tell me that he had worked in a print shop many years ago where the letters were in a block and put in backwards. That way when the page was printed it came out in readable form. He said that when he was baptized in the Holy Spirit that he looked up on the wall and the strange words were set in reverse print. Since he was so accustomed to reading the print backwards he just read the words off the wall and released his spiritual language. Isn't that amazing? Don't be surprised how the Lord will work in your life!

I have learned that Jesus can baptize you anywhere and anytime when you are seeking more of Him and His fullness. When you have that desire to walk in the Spirit and have a power filled life, Jesus will do the work. Oh yes, He can baptize you anyway He wants to. Remember the story when Jesus talked about the boy who asked his father for bread? Did his father give him a stone? Of course not! How much more will the heavenly Father *give the Holy Spirit to those who* ask. You can ask the Father to baptize you anywhere and anytime.

How many times did you have to ask Jesus to forgive your sins and come into your life? Only once! When you pray and ask the Lord to baptize you in the Holy Spirit, will He baptize you? Yes! How many times do you have to ask? Once! We were told we had to tarry but no one knew how long we had to "tarry" and so we just kept seeking this baptism in the Holy Spirit every Sunday night at the altar. It is the same with salvation and with the baptism in the Holy Spirit. Ask and you will receive! When you ask the Father for the "Promise" of this baptism in the Holy Spirit as it reads in Luke 11:13, in the Greek it means you're asking a higher authority.

Be warned, if you are content in your relationship with Jesus and your happy just going to church on Sunday but not reading the Bible or spending time with the Lord. I don't think you will be baptized in the Holy Spirit if you casually or flippantly ask the Lord to baptize you in the Holy Spirit. I know the Lord can do it anyway and you will get ignited for sure. The 120 in the upper room went there expecting. They wanted the promise of the Father and waited for 10 days. I am sure that while they waited they prayed. I don't think they were playing table games or telling jokes. By all indications they were hungry for what the Lord was going to do in their lives. They didn't know exactly how it was going to happen but they waited by faith.

Pastor Bill Chaney made a very interesting statement that I had never heard before but I believe is true. The spiritual language is just part of the package of being baptized in the Holy Spirit. When you ask the Lord to baptize you in the Holy Spirit you can release your language at that time or later as your faith reaches out to speak the words He gives you. So in other words, you do not receive the baptism in the Holy Spirit on one occasion and someday receive your spiritual language because they both come together in the gift just like in Acts 2:4. It is just up to you to be obedient to speak the words that you hear the Spirit giving you even if you don't understand it when those words come to you. You may be doing dishes, in the shower or in your prayer time, get ready!

You might ask people to share specifically how they actually knew what words to speak when they were baptized in the Holy Spirit. Some people hear the words; some just have the words come to their mind and some just start speaking in their spiritual language without even "thinking about it". Some have a syllable; some have a sentence or paragraph and some just start flowing in their language. In fact, I have heard of some who have seen the words and just started reading them like in a vision.

You have to step out in faith and start walking with Jesus. I encourage you to get baptized in water, be in the Word of God and learn to pray to your heavenly Father. Prayer is just talking to God. You also have to step out in faith and start thanking the Lord for baptizing you in the Holy Spirit since you asked Him for this promise of the Father. Do not worry about speaking in tongues. The Lord may do something special just for you so you know that it is the Holy Spirit without a doubt because it will be so unique and not a Jerry Carlson style or like an example in this book!

You will read in some other books also that you may sound like baby talk. You will simply need to learn to use your language and it will grow more and more as you "exercise" it. I started with 2 words, then a week or so later I had a whole sentence. If you lift weights and exercise regularly you gain strength and get better at it. We need to exercise our spiritual language also and "build ourselves up" in our most holy faith. Jude only has 1 chapter and in verses 20-21 it reads, *But you, beloved, building yourselves up on your most holy faith, praying in the Holy Spirit, keep yourselves in the love of God, looking for the mercy of our Lord Jesus Christ unto eternal life.* This is referring to praying in our spiritual language which builds up our faith and I believe prepares us for our day.

Quoting John Amstutz again, "We do not get more of the Holy Spirit, but the Holy Spirit gets more of us". Let Jesus baptize you in His own special way! It will make a difference in your daily walk. Remember this is NOT A BADGE! Quoting Pastor Bill Chaney again, "The baptism in the Holy Spirit doesn't make me holier than you but it makes me better than I was before".

Take time and read 1 Corinthians, chapters 12, 13 and 14. This speaks about your source of power, love and witness! Notice that love in chapter 13, is sandwiched between the gifts of the Spirit in chapters 12 and 14. Love is the Key! This is the kind of love that God pours in us and will pour out of us to touch the world for Him.

Don't worry about anyone else; just make your own choices to walk close to Jesus. We will all stand on our own before God one day to answer for ourselves. Do not seek tongues! Seek more of Jesus! Make Him your Lord and main focus! When you are ready to ask the Father to baptize you in the Holy Spirit then be ready because you may wake up some night speaking in a strange language. That has happened before! One day you will have your own story to tell and share it with others for His glory!

CHAPTER 10
THE GOOD

Now I get to tell you what the "Good" part is of this experience and how the Holy Spirit works in our lives. Oh my, what I have experienced is that I have fallen in love with Jesus and the Word and I started witnessing to people in love rather than in legalism. I have been given a power and authority like I've never had before. This new power to witness with boldness has grown as I have stepped out in faith to speak, share and do things that I never did before. Besides that, I am able to walk in victory more than ever before. No I am not perfect but what a joy to walk in step with Jesus. I am so thankful that this experience has been right inside of me and a daily part of my life for 47 years now.

As I have shared, the Baptism in the Holy Spirit is a one-time event or experience, just like salvation. However, we need to continue to be "filled again" and "refreshed" in the Spirit, just like we need to confess our sins as we live our lives as Christians on a daily basis. We are not getting saved again or getting baptized in the Spirit again, we are simply keeping our lives clean on a daily basis.

Ephesians 5:18 *And do not be drunk with wine, in which is dissipation; but be filled with the Spirit, speaking to one another in psalms and hymns and spiritual songs, singing and making melody in your heart to the Lord.* In the original Greek the verb tense means "continually being filled", since I am a cracked vessel I leak and I need a fresh filling daily! I do not get baptized in the Spirit every day, I just need to "lift weights" by praying in my spiritual language to build up my spiritual muscles.

That's why we need to pray, worship and keep building ourselves up in our most holy faith daily. According to Jude 20 praying *in the spirit* means led by the Spirit or praying in our spiritual language. I need to be built up and receive His divine strength so I can walk in obedience and allow the Lord to work through my life by His power in the Spirit as I walk day by day. Of course I have missed days where I did not pray or worship in my spiritual language, but I did not lose the gifting. I just find I get more accomplished when I spend time with the Lord and I am the one who gets built up when I pray in the Spirit.

Bob Mumford said that each day is a new day and that is why God made night time to separate them. Thank the Lord His mercies are "fresh and new every morning". So try to get in the habit of praying in the Spirit every day so you can walk in the power of the Spirit. He will give you divine appointments and use you in special ways.

Paul and Barnabas were baptized in the Holy Spirit and were empowered by the Spirit to be used in the gifts of the Spirit. Paul wrote in 1 Cor. 14:18 *I thank my God I speak in tongues more than you all.* He told us in verse 39 *Therefore brethren, desire earnestly to prophesy, and do not forbid to speak with tongues. Let all things be done decently and in order.* Paul encourages us here to be used in prophesy.

The Lord can use us to prophesy but there is also the office of a prophet that the Lord will use that person to prophesy or "foretell" future events as revealed to them by the Spirit. The Lord uses most of us to prophesy or "forth tell", utter or declare, things only the Spirit knows to minister to a person or group or a church congregation. So according to 1 Corinthians 14:3 *But he who prophesies speaks edification and exhortation and comfort to men.* The Lord uses us to do this. In other words, our words of prophesy are referred to as "forth telling" or speaking forth or telling forth things in the present. We sense in our spirit that the Holy Spirit is giving us a word or showing us something to build others up. It is to encourage them and to bring comfort as we share that with a person or a Bible study group or with a congregation. Prophesy is nothing like fortune telling, which is not of God.

The Lord started opening up new ministry opportunities for me after we attended a church for a few years. While standing and worshipping the Lord would give me a picture or word for the church congregation so I would pray and ask the Lord if this is just me or Him. I remember that my heart would start pounding and inside I was shaking. I would say, "Lord, if this is from you then let them sing the chorus again" and they did. Or I would say, "Lord, if Tony (our worship leader) starts a time of quiet worship after the chorus then I will go forward". The Lord did!

In the beginning I would go to the pastor and tell them what I saw or heard. That way the pastor, our earthly shepherd, could protect the flock (the congregation) by hearing my message first and making sure it was from the Lord. If the pastor felt it was from the Lord he would hand me the microphone after a worship song finished. After a time, when I had been "tested" the pastor or worship leader just motioned me to come up to the microphone to share what I felt the Lord was saying to the congregation.

Those messages and pictures from the Lord are how I started learning to hear the Lord in another way. It was an exciting time of growth in my life. Don't forget the Holy Spirit is a gentleman and does not interrupt the preaching or a song or a prayer, but He waits for the right timing. Your church may not have anyone come up to share what they believe the Lord is giving them, don't be discouraged. The Lord may use you in your small Bible Study group to start practicing what you believe the Lord is giving you. He may give you a word or picture to share with the group. Other people in the group will confirm your message or give you more direction. He may start using you just to share with one person and that's a good starting point. Keep listening and spending time with Jesus because He wants to use you as His vessel to pour out love, blessings, and encouragement to others!

For example, one Sunday in church during worship I saw in my mind a hand with the other hand cupped over the bottom hand as the Lord was holding a person. I went to the pastor and shared it with him and he said, "Now is not the time, just hold it". I was not offended because I trust him and he is the shepherd over the flock.

The following Sunday the same picture came to me so I went and shared with the pastor again. This time he let me share it in front of the congregation. As I started to share with them I also demonstrated with my hands. I said, "During worship this picture came to me. I saw a hand and it was holding someone in the palm. I saw the other hand cupped over the bottom hand like this." Then I was led by the Spirit to say, "The Lord is not restricting you or imprisoning you. The Lord is holding you and carrying you in the palm of His hand and His other hand is over you to protect you through this season that you're in". Then I sat down.

That week the church received a note from a lady to please thank the person who gave that word from the Lord because she was the one the Lord was speaking to directly. That encouraged my faith to listen more to the Lord and to speak what I believed He was giving to me.

The Word of God is living and powerful as it reads in Hebrews 4:12 *For the word of God is living and powerful, and sharper than any two-edged sword, piercing even to the division of the soul and spirit, and of joints and marrow, and is a discerner of the thoughts and intents of the heart.* The Word of God was written a long time ago and yet it is alive today. That is why you can read a scripture many times but one day it comes alive in you. When the Lord speaks something in a prophetic word of encouragement, it was inspired by the Holy Spirit and it is just as powerful if the Lord uses it again as it was the day the Lord gave that prophetic word.

For example, one night my cousin in Minnesota called me and she had some health issues that were causing some stress and anxiety. I prayed for her over the phone and that same picture came to me from years ago. So I spoke it over her in my prayer that the Lord's hand was holding her and His other hand was covering her to protect her as she walked through this season. I also prayed for His peace to rest on her and for her body to function as the Lord created it. I prayed whatever the Lord was bringing to my mind, including speaking to the enemy in the authority and powerful name of Jesus that he was to go to Jesus to be judged by Jesus and go where Jesus tells him to go, that he has no authority or influence in her life. When I finished praying she said, "Jerry, as you were praying I felt like God had a big magnet and He was just pulling those things out of me." Thank You Lord! That's not me; I was just doing what I felt led to do by the Spirit! When the Spirit inspires something, it is alive no matter how old it is! Now you see why the work of the Spirit in the book of Acts is still working today.

Remember Peter and others reported all that God had done through their ministry and not for their own pride. I am amazed that God can use me but He loves to use mankind and none of us are perfect. So it is only by the power of the Holy Spirit that lives are touched for Jesus, not by our own wisdom, our power or speaking skills, and definitely not by my writing skills.

What did Jesus say? You shall receive power to become witnesses. When you witness you just share what God has done in your life and it does not put that person on the defense. They listen and can accept or reject your sharing about Jesus in your life. The Holy Spirit will use you to plant a seed, water a seed or reap the harvest by leading them to Jesus. It's not up to us to convert anyone, the Holy Spirit will do that as we are witnesses to what Jesus has done in our lives. It is only up to us to love them.

The Holy Spirit speaks through me by bringing a thought to my mind that I had no knowledge of. For example, as I was teaching at a recent Men's Retreat on this subject, I used a little wooden cross I carved and mounted to a base as a visual aid. As I was using the water glasses about big sin and little sin with the pitcher of water nearby, I said something to the effect, "I don't care if you're the best person on this earth, the worse criminal there ever was or a Hell's Angel, we are all equal at the foot of the cross".

Never had I ever thought of using the words "Hell's Angel" in all my years of teaching but this was the Holy Spirit giving me these words because He knew who was in the class. I was actually surprised that came out of my mouth. After the class a guy came up and said he had been with the Hell's Angels and had accepted Christ into his life but now he wanted to be baptized in the Holy Spirit. Those words came to me by the Holy Spirit just for that one man. I didn't have time to even think about it, the words just came out.

During this time of writing this book I was praying for a person one morning and a picture came to my mind. When I have these words, thoughts, pictures or other things come to me I contact that person to tell them about it. This is what I said, "John, this is what came to me so this might just be me, or it may be the Holy Spirit. If it speaks to your heart and your spirit bears witness then great. If it does not then just disregard what I am about to share with you".

That person had shared a situation with me at a previous time so I was praying for him when this picture came to my mind. I told him "I saw you taking a sheet of paper and drawing a line down the center. On the top left column you wrote a plus (+) sign and on top of the right column you put a minus (-) sign. Then I saw you writing in detail the things that are positive and negative about that _____. Then I saw you fold the paper in half down the middle, with the negative things on the backside and the positive things on the front facing you." I also told him to put the negative things behind him and focus on the positive in front of him about that situation. He thanked me for my call.

We don't always know what the Lord is showing us or wants us to share. Maybe the Lord used someone else to call him and add something else on the same topic. Or maybe in a sermon or in a song the Holy Spirit will bring it to light and it all comes together for him. Remember, the results are up to the Lord, not you or me! We are just to be obedient to what we hear the Lord speaking or showing us.

Some people may wonder "Where is the boldness of the Spirit in you? Why are you so timid when you share what the Lord gives you? You should tell them that God told you to say it". I know that if the person is not ready to hear it, they can disregard it even if it was from the Lord. But I also know if I heard the Lord then the Holy Spirit will keep bringing that picture or word back to their mind until they can receive it. I don't need to say "The Lord told me to tell you". That can make a person defensive so I let the Holy Spirit do the work in their lives.

Also beware, if you tell someone, "The Lord spoke to me and said to tell you _____". By saying that, you are placing them in a position where they feel like God is speaking and they do not have any decision in the matter. If you were speaking out of the flesh and thinking God told you something to tell them, you may be totally off track. They may know you are off track or you could cause them to make a terrible decision, thinking God was speaking to them.

Be careful when you think you have a word from the Lord for someone. You can do more damage than good. Make sure it is the Holy Spirit speaking to you and He will confirm the message to them. Hopefully they will wait to get confirmation from 1 or 2 more sources. You must be in the Word because He can use you to speak scriptures into their life and He will change that person or give them direction by His words instead of just your words.

Hebrews 4:12 in the Amplified Classic Version (AMPC) *For the Word that God speaks is alive and full of power [making it active, operative, energizing, and effective]: it is sharper than any two-edged sword, penetrating to the dividing line of the breath of life (soul) and [the immortal] spirit, and of joints and marrow [of the deepest parts of our nature], exposing and sifting and analyzing and judging the very thoughts and purposes of the heart.*

When I get prompted by the Spirit or have a thought come to my mind, I would rather fail trying to be obedient to the Spirit than not to obey at all. I try to walk by faith and trust the Lord. Oh yes, I pray and try to test my thoughts to make sure I am hearing the Lord. Sometimes I test it through my wife because she is a woman of God and can give me wise Godly counsel.

Earlier I spoke about the importance of being in the Word daily and memorizing it. That way the Holy Spirit can speak to you and give you the scriptures to share with others that may change their life. I was just reminded of an incident back in the 1970s. I was working in the Portland area and our friends had moved there from Fresno so I had their address with me. The lead investigator in Seattle asked me to go to another town to get court records. If you don't know it, there is not one straight street outside of the downtown area of Portland. I was driving on those curvy roads and saw their street name so I turned around and to my surprise their home was about 5 houses down the street. I knocked on the door and the wife came to the door. As we talked for about 5 minutes she was so negative about their move to Oregon.

The next morning in the hotel room I was having my time in the Word and prayer. I had these thoughts come to my mind about her so I wrote them down and I felt the Lord gave me two scriptures to give to her. I said to the Lord, "Oh Lord, these are heavy scriptures; I can't give these to her and say what you are asking me to tell her on the phone. Lord I have no idea if I will ever see her again". The investigator in Seattle called me right after my time with the Lord and said, "Jerry, I hate to ask you to do this but can you go back to (that same town) and get some more information?" Of course, I was glad to! Thank you Jesus, You are so amazing! He makes a way when He wants to get His work done and He uses mankind most of the time. Sometimes He uses angels but most of the time he uses imperfect clay vessels and sometimes He even uses non-believers who have no clue that God is using them.

Finding my way is one of my strengths and if I have been to a place once, I can find it years later. That was before GPS, whether in the mountains, a city, in the day or night. The Portland area is the worse place to find any address. I had no clue if I would find their home but somehow I ended up taking a turn on a country road and was going past their street again. I think the Lord confused me on that trip to find their home. I turned around and went back and I knocked on the door and guess who answered it, the wife.

I said, "You know when I saw you yesterday you were so down and negative about having moved here. I have something to tell you and it won't be easy to hear". I told her how I felt that I could not give her this word over the phone but when the investigator asked me to return to that courthouse for more information, I ended up here again. I then told her, "I think I have some scriptures for you that came to me while I was having my time with the Lord this morning and I have some words for you but they are really heavy!" She immediately said, "Jerry, I know you, give me what the Lord spoke to you". So I gave her the paper with the scriptures and the words I felt the Lord gave me. She thanked me and I left.

That Christmas we saw that couple when they were visiting in Fresno at a mutual friend's home. Her husband, who had not accepted Christ yet, came to me and said, "Jerry I don't know what you said to my wife when you were in Oregon but when I came home from work that day she was a different woman". He came to the Lord shortly after that and ended up as a deacon at a church. Is that God or what? The Lord loves us and cares about each one of us! See how important it is that we are in the Word daily? I challenge you to memorize the Word and get it in your mind. The Holy Spirit will take the written word and bring it to life in your Spirit someday to minister to you, or to use it to minister to someone else.

In 1980, a lady who had an intimate relationship with the Lord and knew His voice was obedient to the Holy Spirit. One day she heard from the Holy Spirit, but what He spoke to her didn't make any sense to her at all. So here is the story.

On October 17, 1980, we had no food left in the house when we got up that morning. We went through about 2 years of financial struggle because of my use of the credit card to finish our new home. When we woke up that morning Barbara said we can't send the boys to school with nothing to eat. The Holy Spirit brought to my mind the scripture I had memorized in Romans 14:17, *For the kingdom of God is not eating and drinking, but righteousness and peace and joy in the Holy Spirit.* I grabbed her hand and told her, "Yes we can, the Lord will provide!"

We woke the boys up and I asked them if they could go to school without breakfast or lunch, but not tell anyone. They were about 8 and 10 years old and they said, "Sure dad we can go on the playground at lunch time and no one will know we didn't eat". I told them that the Lord would provide. Their faith through that season was amazing. I told them on the way home after church on Sundays that someday we would get to go to McDonalds.

Well my friend, the Lord provided miraculously that day. Another amazing story of God speaking and directing a life that walks with Him. That lady felt led to stop at the grocery store before going to the ladies Bible study. Well that lady stopped at a grocery store but she told the Lord that she didn't need anything. She went inside, got a basket and went up and down isles and bought groceries that she didn't even like or want as she felt prompted by the Spirit to take things off the shelf.

When the ladies started to have donuts and coffee Barbara refused to eat since her boys had nothing to eat that morning.

They kept pressuring her until Barbara started crying and told them what happened. The lady said, "Okay that is why the Lord had me stop and get the groceries". She went out to her car and the groceries were everything the boys liked, the bread, the meat, the chips and more. A lunch was taken to school for them that day.

Here is the rest of the story. The Lord showed me in a dream the night before the home that lady and her husband lived in east of town and I had never been there. She had fixed dinner for me, and for 4 other couples. What was so weird in the dream was that when dinner was ready they had me sit down to eat but the others were just standing around the table watching me and were so happy for me. I didn't understand the dream that morning but Barbara told me what happened when I got home from work. I knew that dream was from the Lord showing me He would provide since I represented my family when I was being fed at her table.

That was on a Friday. On Sunday I asked that lady if she lived in a little white house east of Clovis with a white picket fence. Yes she did! See what God can do when a person spends time in the Word and in His presence? He speaks to us and shows us things even in the night. The Lord gave me encouragement by the Word I memorized and the Lord used her to minister to us as the "Spirit led her". Thank the Lord for people who walk in the Spirit and are sensitive to His leading. I cannot emphasize that enough and I desire to be sensitive to the Spirit every day. Oh I could tell you more stories for sure!

The Lord wants to give you something to minister to your life and to minister through your life to others. In First Corinthians 13:9 it reads that, *For we know in part and we prophesy in part.* That is why it is good to be in a group of people who love the Lord and are walking in the Spirit. The Lord can speak to several people and give greater clarity to the topic instead of just one person having "the whole picture" or "the whole message". Sometimes one person may have the whole message the Lord wants to deliver.

Oh, I wish I had learned to ask the Holy Spirit questions after I was baptized in the Holy Spirit but I never had any training or mentoring about walking in the Spirit. I have been learning more of how He wants to help me to be a better witness. Here are a few examples of what I have learned over the last 40 years and I am still learning.

This was possibly one of those first times when I was in Highpoint North Carolina at the ticket counter when I noticed a cowboy with a Stetson hat. My attention was just drawn to him as the Lord normally does but I wasn't given a specific word or direction for him. This was back over 40 years ago before I learned to ask the Lord what to ask them. I was in my seat and he sat down across the aisle and forward 2 seats. He got up to put his Stetson in the overhead when another guy came in and sat in his seat. He turned around and told the guy to go ahead and sit there and came and sat next to me. He said he and the other guy were both flying standby so they were the last ones on the plane. He told me that he was scheduled to fly out 2 days before, to attend a rodeo and to go buy some horses in Colorado. I shared Jesus with him and I got to pray with him on the plane for the assurance of his salvation. I asked him, "Is this a divine appointment or what? You were going to fly out 2 days ago and then you came today and you gave up your seat to sit next to me". He agreed that it was definitely an appointment set up by the Lord.

About 40 years ago I was changing flights from Atlanta to Greensboro and a young lady came and sat in the aisle seat. I was at the window and there was an empty seat between us. I greeted her, but she was not in a friendly mood. She sat down and had her shoulder turned away from me. I thought, "she does not want to talk". This may have been one of the first times I asked the Holy Spirit what I should ask someone. So I asked the Holy Spirit and He brought to my mind, "Ask her if she has anyone praying for her". I literally responded to the

Lord in my mind, "Wow, I would never have thought of that! That is awesome!"

When we were up in the air I turned and asked her, "Excuse me can I ask you a question?" She turned to look over her right shoulder and said okay. I said, "Do you have anyone praying for you?" Wow her eyes got big as saucers and she said, "Oh yes, I have a lot of people praying for me". I said, "That's great, do you love Jesus?" and she said yes in a very non-committed tone of voice. I said that's great and then it was like the Holy Spirit just gave me the "cut it" sign, like my finger across my throat. In other words, CUT IT-NO MORE. Don't say another word to her. I started thinking, Lord, she is either running away from you and people are praying for her, or she has never surrendered to you and people are praying for her. I think the Lord put me right there in that seat to remind her that God knew right where she was and He loved her.

As a federal agent I would get sent on top priority calls when a government employee was threatened or assaulted for example. So anytime I go to the airport I start looking for the next person the Lord wants me to speak to. One time in the 70s I was going on an assault case in Reno and I was standing in line at the ticket counter. A young couple was standing in the front of the line. For some reason the girl was drawn to my attention (that is normally what the Lord will do, He will draw my attention to a specific person). When we went to the plane, she kissed the guy goodbye and got on the plane. I ended up sitting behind her and I don't know how but I started talking to her over her seat back.

She had a hunger for the Lord so I asked her if I could come up and sit next to her. She was hungry to know more about the baptism in the Holy Spirit and I got to share with her for an hour before we landed. How did that happen? Another one of my mottos is if I feel the Lord prompting me to do or say something "JUST DO IT". I'd rather fail trying to obey than not to obey at all, have you heard that before?

I was changing planes in Dallas in September 2019, and a man was sitting in front of me. However, two people came in and either they wanted to sit together or he was in the wrong seat. Either way the Lord had him move next to me in the small plane. I met Michael who was going to Springfield to speak at an Insurance Conference. Barbara and I were going to a Vietnam Sentry Dog Handler reunion in Springfield. I asked the Lord what I should ask him. The Lord brought to my mind "Ask him if he has been thinking about heaven". I turned to ask him and he had his headphones on and eyes closed so I waited. When the snacks were brought he ordered some drinks and we took time to eat.

I turned to him and I said, "Michael, have you been thinking about heaven?" Wow, his eyes got so big and he looked at me and said, "Jerry, I have been thinking about heaven ever since I got on the plane in Phoenix". I don't remember if I asked him if he knew how to get to heaven or if I just started sharing Jesus like I normally do.

Do you remember the triangle I drew and had you put God's name in it and then your name in the second triangle? Well, I drew the triangles on a napkin and explained it to Michael as I shared about the Father, Son and Holy Spirit and then wrote "God" in the middle. Then I drew another triangle and wrote body, soul and spirit on the corners, then I wrote Michael's name in the middle. I explained how God created him in God's image and for relationship with Him. I told Michael how much God loved him and he had great value to the Lord since God sent His Son Jesus to die on a cross for his sins, then Jesus rose from the dead to give him eternal life. That is a great witnessing tool.

Michael was totally focused as I explained how our spirit is dead before being born again and how our soul is made up of our mind, will and emotions. Before accepting Christ people try to figure God out with their mind or their great intellect and it is all foolishness to them. Our will does what we want and our emotions can control us. When we repent and ask

Jesus for forgiveness then our spirit is born again and becomes alive. After being born again our minds are being renewed by the Word of God and by the Spirit. Now our will wants to please the Lord but we still have to guard our emotions.

After I explained all those things to Michael I asked him if he would like to ask Jesus Christ to forgive his sins, come into his life and make Jesus Lord of his life. Michael replied, "Jerry, yes I want to because I need to get my life together but I want to do it when I am sober. I knew I shouldn't have ordered those drinks. Give me that napkin with all your notes. I want to keep that with me". So I gave him the napkin and my name and contact information. I have not heard from him yet, but that's okay, I just pray he will surrender to Jesus as I pray for everyone I witness to. Is God amazing? The Holy Spirit knows what people are thinking!

After we left the Dog Handler reunion in Springfield, we went to St. Louis to see the Arch where I tried to get hired as an Iron Worker back in the 60s when it was just getting off the ground. I was in a hotel having breakfast in the dining room. An older gentleman was vacuuming the floor and I was trying to hear the TV weather report regarding the storms that were coming. I was ticked off at him and wished he would turn it off or go work in another room. But no, he just kept vacuuming. I inhaled my food and went back to my room rather unhappy.

Barb was sitting in the chair having her quiet time with the Lord and I jumped up on the bed. I opened my Bible to read in the Old Testament. I opened it to Amos chapter 7 and as I got to verse 8, where Amos writes, *And the Lord said to me, "Amos what do you see?"* Just as I read that the Holy Spirit asked me, "Jerry what do you see?" I probably hung my head and said, "I see that man in the dining room. Okay Lord, what do you want me to ask him?" The Lord put this thought in my mind, "Ask him if he is ready to go to heaven".

As I got off the bed Barbara asked me where I was going. In a rather humble and maybe grumbly voice I said "I'm going to go and see a man in the dining room". I walked in as he was sweeping and I introduced myself. I asked him, "William, are you ready to go to heaven?" He said, "Oh yes sir, I believe in God even though I don't go to church but I have lived a good life" and on and on he went.

Then I shared with him briefly how believing in God won't get you to heaven, the Bible says that the demons believe in God and they tremble (James 2:19). Being a good person will not get you to heaven because it is not by your good works so you can't boast about that (Ephesians 2:8-9). After sharing briefly with him about what Christ had done for him, and I didn't even use the triangle drawings, I ended up asking William if he wanted to ask Jesus Christ to forgive him of his sins and ask Jesus to be Lord of his life. William put the broom aside and reached out and took both my hands in his hands as I prayed with him to accept Christ's forgiveness.

In my mind I knew I was supposed to give him my business card so I got it and went back to the dining room. Sometimes the Lord will use something, like the napkin with my notes, or a business card or something as a tool to remind that person of their encounter with Jesus, when the Lord uses us to speak to them. As I walked into the dining room I said, "William" and he stopped sweeping and looked up at me. I lifted my right hand to heaven and pointed and said, "Thank you Jesus!". William put the broom in his left hand and pointed to heaven with his right hand and said, "Thank you Jesus!" Then he came to me and hugged me and said thank you. He told me everything he was going through in cancer treatments and he shared about his serious health situation. Thank you Jesus! The Lord knows right where people are and what they need to hear! William was not the same man that came to the hotel to work that morning.

A few months ago I was at Chic Filet eating outside and a young man with a back pack sat down at a nearby table. I felt the Holy Spirit prompt me to ask him if he was running from the Lord. So after I ate I went to his table and asked him how he was doing. Then I said, "It looks like your traveling with your backpack" and he said yes. Then I asked him, "Are you running from God?" Oh wow, his response showed me he did not like that question and did not want to talk about it. I wished him safe travels in a kind way and left. Then I thought, Oh Lord he knows that You know right where he is and You will not leave him alone!

You do not have to be an evangelist in order to share Jesus or tell someone your testimony or lead someone to Jesus. No matter who you are, God will use you in your own special way! In fact, you may not want to witness like I do. I went to the hospital to see my friend Bob and he was not in the room. I asked the man in the next bed where Bob was and he had no idea since he came into an empty room. I introduced myself and asked about his health situation. Then I asked him if he took his last breath right now did he know where he would go? I ended up praying with him to rededicate his life to Christ. I have done that in airplanes also but I wasn't trying to scare them. That is just what the Holy Spirit brought to my mind at that time. Well, he started coming to our church and his wife came and gave her life to Christ. You see, God even works through ways that are not "normal" or "correct".

There are so many things God has done in my life and the lives of others, even as John said at the end of his writing in the gospel of John verse 21:25 *And there are also many other things that Jesus did, which if they were written one by one, I suppose that even the world itself could not contain the books that would be written. Amen.* I say AMEN to that!

I have a friend Dale that was in the hospital a few years ago. The doctors were concerned that he may have cancer because of a blockage in his colon. I wanted to go and visit him on a Wednesday to pray for Dale. I was not the only one who went to see Dale because other men had gone to see him. Those men laid hands on Dale, anointed him with oil and prayed for his healing also. Here is an example of several people praying for someone's healing.

I asked him how he was and he told me the problem. I asked Dale if I could lay hands on his abdomen and pray for him and he said yes. So I did that and prayed for his healing. I did not feel "Holy Ghost goose bumps" or any other feelings, I just pray for healing because I know God heals! As I prayed I said that the doctors would not find any cancer, the blockage would open and he would be released from the hospital Friday morning. That even shocked me that I said "he would be released Friday morning".

Well, Dale told me later that the doctor came in just before noon on Friday and asked Dale if he wanted to see the x-rays of his abdomen. The x-rays showed that Dale was totally clear, no blockage and no cancer. He would have been released from the hospital Friday morning before noon as the Holy Spirit directed me to say but the doctor wanted to keep him one more night for observation. Now was that the Lord? That is another example of the prompting by the Holy Spirit to speak something that I did not know in myself.

I want to expand on what I shared earlier how the Lord speaks to us. I told you about the "internal audible voice" that Jack Deere teaches on. No one else can hear it, it is not audible, but we can hear those words that are spoken to us by the Spirit and they are as clear as a bell. Our everyday walk with the Lord helps us to be sensitive when God prompts or nudges us to say or do something through the Holy Spirit. There are times when the Lord speaks audibly to someone but it is not a daily encounter. There are other times the Lord can use a prophetic word and there are times when the Lord will use circumstances to speak to us or guide us and give us direction.

There are specific times that the Lord has spoken to me and given me correction in that internal audible voice that is so clear and powerful. I can think of about 7 times that the Lord spoke so strongly to me that way. I knew it was the Lord speaking to me and it was definitely not a God nudge or a thought the Holy Spirit brought to my mind!

It may have been about 1990, I had this great idea to try and remember how many people I have prayed with to accept Jesus in their life. So I got out paper and a pen and before I could put one drop of ink on the paper the Holy Spirit spoke to me and said, "Don't count the notches on your gun". Wow, that was a check for me! I put that pen down fast! The Lord speaks to us in ways we understand but someone else may not understand the words He speaks to us.

I met John Burns, the Director of Central Valley Teen Challenge, the spring of 2014, at church. Barbara and I were both familiar with the Teen Challenge Ministry since we were kids in 1958, when it was founded by David Wilkerson in New York City. John was repairing the 75 year old building complex in Reedley hoping to open in October 2015. I started praying, "Lord I want to teach at Teen Challenge". I never said a word to John or the pastor. I just kept praying and begging God to let me teach at that adult men's campus. I had already learned that the Lord knows my name, my address and even my cell phone number! I know to wait on Him and not force myself into a ministry or anything. So I just kept waiting and praying, and begging.

In January of 2016, I took my little travel trailer up the mountain to spend some time alone with the Lord. On Thursday morning, January 7, I was begging and pleading with God to please let me teach at Teen Challenge. The Holy Spirit spoke to me in that internal audible voice and He said it so forcefully, as if He raised His voice like He was fed up with my begging and pleading and crying like a little kid, "BE STILL AND KNOW THAT I AM GOD". YIKES! Another correction. I don't think those words would be classed as direction for me, just correcting me again.

Twenty-eight days later I got a phone call from John asking me to meet him for lunch. We had never met for lunch or visited at church so I wasn't asking him how things were going at the campus or with the ministry. He said that he was praying and felt the Lord gave him my name to be on the Advisory Board. What? And yet I knew immediately that was what the Lord was preparing me for. I never told him I wanted to teach.

In November we were meeting with a judge. After our meeting he saw a handout I was using to share and mentor a young man at the Reedley campus on Saturdays. After looking at my handout titled "The Price of Unforgiveness" He said, "Jerry you can teach at Chapel next Wednesday". Oh the joy! Later he asked me to start teaching classes in January 2017. The Lord knows our heart's desires but sometimes He waits until we are ready or obedient to Him so He can use us. Be obedient in the small things first, and then see where God takes you!

In 2017, I was praying and worshipping in my little 8'x10' log cabin in the back yard. As I was praying in the Spirit it seemed it was more than me just praying, it was more like the Lord was giving me special words in the Spirit. It felt like it was a message in tongues so I asked the Holy Spirit, "If this is a message in tongues please give me the interpretation". I wrote down the words that started coming to my mind.

At noon I went to Central Valley Teen Challenge to teach my 2 classes. I was surprised that one of the men had to leave and that was his last day in my class. I prayed for him and as I was praying the Holy Spirit told me that the message I received in the cabin was for him. So right there in my Holy Spirit class I was able to explain to the class how the Lord spoke to me while worshipping in my spiritual language that morning. I told the class how I felt that my language had changed and I thought it might be a message in tongues. At that point I asked the Lord if it was a message in tongues to please give me the interpretation. I got the paper out and shared with him the words the Lord had given me. I read the words to him in front of the other men and gave the paper to take with him. That was a practical teaching lesson for sure and a new experience for me. God can do anything! Have I said that before?

How I would love to sit down and hear what the Lord is doing in your life. He has done so many things in my life I could write another book on the stories.

Get ready when you seek the Lord and get to know Him but never forget it is more important that He "knows you"! I never want to hear the words "depart from Me I never knew you". I cannot stress it enough; make Jesus Christ the Lord of your life! Then be ready as the Lord will start speaking to you and using you in special ways.

CHAPTER 11
THE BAD

Did you ever think anyone would tell you bad things that can happen as a result of someone being baptized in the Holy Spirit? Well, I'm giving you some things to think about and to guard against, as well as maybe a word of caution that you can share with someone else at some point in time.

These are things that I have become aware of but still do not have all the answers. I hope this helps you understand why some people who are "Christians", "Spirit filled" or "baptized in the Holy Spirit and speak in tongues" still do things that may not reflect Christ in their life.

They may be new believers or those who have been baptized in the Holy Spirit. My brother's high school friend got saved one weekend and the following Friday night he went back to a place he had always gone before. His friends asked him, "What are you doing here? You are supposed to be a Christian now". Even the unbelievers know how Christians should act and what they should not do!

When it comes to the baptism in the Holy Spirit and I'm teaching a class, I specifically caution people about this free gift. When a person gets baptized in the Holy Spirit they can get so "on fire" to be in church, a prayer meeting or some church worship meeting that they can cause relational stress with family members simply because of their zeal for the Lord.

As an example for married families, the husband and kids might be ready to have breakfast before going to work and school but mom had already left for an early morning prayer meeting, totally forgetting to fix breakfast. Then there is the issue of the husband or wife that wants to go to a Bible study or to church on Sunday, and the spouse and kids have other plans. Now what should they do? God comes first right?

If the spouse is not happy about you leaving or being gone, respond to them in a loving way as Jesus asks us to. Respect your spouse, honor them and ask them if you can go to the prayer meeting, to church or Bible study. Then respond to them in love no matter what their answer is.

Your actions and body language speaks louder than your words, so show them that you are okay with their decision and that it does not make you mad or upset. Maybe you need to have a good attitude and stay with them and spend the evening together. Can you imagine how a spouse feels now that you have become a "Christian", "Charismaniac" or "Holy Roller" or whatever they call you? What really throws them a curve is when you visibly change and become more respectful towards them. You show them love in tangible ways and honor them in what they ask you to do or not do.

Love, honor and respect is what makes a big difference as you allow Jesus to shine through your life. What about 1 Peter 3 verses 1 and 2 where it states that the husband may be won by the wife's behavior without any words (of preaching at them). This is the ultimate goal that the spouse comes into their own personal relationship with Jesus.

In verse 7 the man is to honor the wife as a joint heir of the grace of life so his prayers aren't hindered. Maybe she is not a believer yet, but your life may bring her to a place where she accepts Jesus. Don't forget to read the rest of 1 Peter chapter 3 as it shows how to act and live and what the Lord likes. Verses 8 to 12 states in essence to love each other, be compassionate, don't repay evil for evil or insult with insult but give a blessing so you will inherit a blessing. Then it shares what the Lord wants from us and that His face is turned against those who do evil.

As I said before, when a young person or spouse comes to Christ or gets baptized in the Holy Spirit, the enemy does not like it. The enemy will try to bring division in the home, start arguments and try to wreak havoc. The enemy tries to do the same with relatives and in churches. If you are struggling in your marriage relationship, please remember that God puts opposites together so we can grow. Your spouse is not your enemy, the enemy of our soul is trying to stir things up and destroy marriages!

Have you ever argued with your spouse on Sunday mornings before going to church? When you get to church you put on your happy face as you get out of the car. We have never done that! Oh yeah? Let me count the times years ago. Let me tell you the devil will finally give up once he sees you are determined to love Jesus, love each other and you are going to church no matter what happens. Hang in there!

You can also tell the devil to get out of your house or car and go to the feet of Jesus to be judged by Jesus because he has no more influence in your life or in your home. You have that authority in Jesus Christ.

Another bad thing that can happen after a person gets saved or baptized in the Holy Spirit is if this person gets angry and starts to argue or give reasons why they should be allowed to go to church or a meeting. What is also bad and can cause more problems is when a spouse tells the other one they "need to get saved" or other remarks that do not reflect Christ. It is NOT our job to convert anyone. We are only to let Christ shine through our life and the fruit of the Spirit be evident as we read in Galatians 5:22-23.

Isn't it interesting that the first fruit of the Spirit is love? Once you've lost love, you've lost your joy, then you lose all peace and you're not longsuffering. Shall I go on? Get the picture?

We should only share Jesus in a loving way, which means through our daily life and testimony. Love is the key! Arguing, accusing, preaching and being mean to that spouse or parent will not reflect Christ and it will end up driving a wedge in your relationship which is the goal of the enemy. Paul asked the church at Corinth, 1 Corinthians 4:21 ...*Shall I come to you with a rod, or in love and a spirit of gentleness?* Watch how this makes the big difference in representing Christ.

Now for the rest of my story. I have shared this in classes that I teach and now I get to put in into print as a word of warning. This is another example of what bad things can result from being baptized in the Holy Spirit or in your walk with the Lord. Please don't let this happen to you!

As I said, I was baptized in the Holy Spirit on Sunday night, February 11, 1973. I started a deeper walk in the Spirit and the Lord started working in my life and through my life, it was amazing. If someone had a headache, I would pray and it would leave. In fact, we did not even have aspirins in our home because I would just pray and God would heal. Back in those days we only had aspirins as the only cure for headaches and pain. Back in the 1970s I had migraine headaches. In fact, I remember having severe headaches back in my college years in the 1960s. When I woke up I felt a headache starting, but instead of staying in bed, I went to work anyway at the Treasury office. Before noon the headache was so bad that I would leave work and got sick on the side of the road driving home.

One time I was driving home with a migraine and heading north on Peach approaching McKinley by the Fresno Airport, I had a thought come to me. I thought "Lord when I lay hands on people sometimes you heal them". So I laid a hand on my forehead as I was driving and asked the Lord to heal me. I turned east on McKinley then north on Clovis Avenue heading home. By the time I got home the Lord had healed me and the migraine headache was gone.

That is an example of what the Lord was doing in my life. I had the honor of witnessing and leading people to Christ as well as praying for healing. Then I became very prideful again. I never said it but my thoughts were, "Where is your faith? I just pray and the Lord heals". My thoughts and pride didn't stop there, in fact, I thought, "We don't even have aspirins in

130

our house, I pray and God heals so where's your faith?" Oh how the enemy can come and sneak in and lay traps for us any time and any way he can. I never even realized that I had become a "Spirit Filled Tongue Talk'n Pharisee". I was so judgmental and critical of everyone else and their lack of faith.

In 1979, I walked into the dining room and looked over the half-wall into the living room where Barbara was watching a Christian program on the television. The man was interviewing Vicki Jamison. Vicki sang a song and people got healed. In that very moment as I walked into the room I heard Vicki say, "I asked the Lord how come when I sing You only heal some people and You do not heal everyone? The Holy Spirit spoke to me and said, ""All I want you to do is love them"".

When she said that, the Holy Spirit convicted me of my pride and arrogance and I fell on my face weeping for at least 20 minutes right there on the dining room floor. It's all about the love, not my ability! The Holy Spirit is such a gentleman, long suffering and patient. Oh how I wish He would just use a 2X4 on my head sometimes. But no, He comes in a gentle way and reveals things that are not pleasing to the Father. He waits for the right timing, otherwise I won't hear Him.

That was the first step by the Holy Spirit to break my pride. The second major time is when we were at Peoples Church, in Fresno, California. We were in a 32 week Lay Leadership training class in 1980 with 16 other couples. At the end of the meeting one Sunday afternoon, we were all kneeling in a circle and praying. The Lord showed me a vision of me climbing a ladder. I was looking up through a cloud and I thought I could see another rung so I would reach up through the cloud and sure enough there was another rung. As I pulled myself up it became clear and then I thought I could see another rung through the cloud. Sure enough there was a rung and I would reach for it and start to pull myself up and it became clear. This only happened for about 3 rungs and it only took a few seconds for this vision. I didn't tell anyone about it. I began to think about it and I asked the Lord what it meant.

My feet were on the lower rungs which were the basic fundamentals of faith like believing God raised Jesus from the dead; repentance; salvation; water baptism; prayer; reading the Word; fasting and memorizing the Word for examples. As I looked up I saw another rung and the Lord revealed another area in my life that I needed to grow in. If I had stopped looking up and just focused on the rung that I was holding onto, I might have believed that rung was the best thing ever, and I would have missed more things that the Lord had for me. Sometimes we can get stuck on a rung.

For example a construction worker was out Friday night getting drunk with his buddies and chasing women. Maybe on Saturday he was on the bottom rung of the ladder with the Holy Spirit drawing him to Christ. On Sunday he went to church and got saved. Now on Monday morning he wanted all his work buddies to get saved. He was excited about his new life and he is focused on the salvation rung of the ladder. That is all he can talk about to everyone. As he starts to grow in the Lord and look up the ladder he will see the Lord has more for him to learn and grow in.

When someone gets baptized in water they are so excited they go around asking if their family and friends have been baptized in water. They can be a little bit obnoxious and insensitive in their new found joy. Here they are stuck on the rung of water baptism for a while.

Have you ever been in a season of intercessory prayer and wondered why the church wasn't having prayer meetings at 5:00 AM every day of the week? I've been there and done that, and I was critical of the pastor in my heart for not having prayer meetings every day. I never said anything back in those days.

Were you involved in a ministry where you got so self-focused that you thought everyone should be involved in it too? We can get stuck on that rung and judge others who are not on the same rung that we are on. I am on the ministry rung of Central Valley Teen Challenge but I have matured and I know that it is not the only ministry in the world. Thank the Lord that there are other ministries like Pregnancy Care Center and prison ministries for two examples.

It is critical that we continue to look up to Jesus so He can continue to work in our lives so we can get to know Him and understand Him more. The Lord delights in us knowing and understanding Him as I have shared previously in Jeremiah 9:23-24. You can't wait to get in your secret place with Him.

Back to the vision... I started to think about the two boards on each side of the ladder holding the rungs together. I thought that one must be faith and the other one must be worship. Then the Holy Spirit spoke to me and said, "No, the rungs are held together with love, and love is the key". He reminded me of that when, over the next few weeks our Sunday school teacher taught us about love. Then the pastor's sermon was on love. God wanted to make sure it sunk in my thick skull.

The Holy Spirit spoke to me again and said "Never judge or criticize where someone else is on their spiritual ladder, and remember love is the key". All the Lord wants us to do is to love others! That was the second major thing that the Holy Spirit did to start breaking pride in me.

I need to share this verse again... John 13:34-35, Jesus was speaking, *A new commandment I give to you, that you love one another; as I have loved you, that you also love one another. By this all will know that you are my disciples, if you have love for one another.*

Jesus never encouraged us to criticize and judge one another. I have heard it said that only Christians devour their wounded. Isn't that a sad statement? If someone falls into sin and instead of restoring them that person is ostracized or put out of the church. What a sad commentary for those of us who are supposed to represent Christ. I felt that way when I was a Pharisee but I have seen two churches I have attended that have restored wounded sheep, which is God's heart!

When a person is raised in legalism and being around critical and judgmental attitudes, it is hard to break that on our own because it is so engrained in our upbringing. I still battle when my flesh wants to sit on the throne of my life instead of allowing the Holy Spirit to be on the throne. The Holy Spirit is still working in me to make me what I ought to be! Oh how I need Jesus to continue to work in my life!

A retired Treasury Agent friend called me one day after I retired. He said, "Jerry you are a man of many titles". Wow, that started the wheels turning. I prayed and asked the Lord to humble me but about 10 years later I realized James 4:10 tells us to humble ourselves. I started letting go of titles. I resigned my position as an investigator on contract with the federal government. I closed my business, and I also stopped the monthly breakfast meetings for law enforcement and private investigators. I stepped down from the prayer team and other positions. Then I took off all of my titles from my email address and now I just have my name and phone number. I've already told you about when I picked up the broken glass on the sidewalk a few years ago. Isn't it amazing how the Lord can use simple circumstances to teach us something? Just a little broken bottle is all it took to open my eyes again. He loves us so much and keeps drawing us to Him.

James 4:10 also reminds us that the Lord will lift us up or exalt us which means He can call us into serving or into a position of leadership in His timing. The end of the verse in the Amplified Classic Version reads ...*and He will exalt you [He will lift you up and make your lives significant]*. That doesn't mean to lift us up or exalt us for pride sake. It wasn't long and the Lord started using me shortly after I laid it all down. Our new Pastor Bill Chaney knew nothing about me and yet the Lord spoke to him to ask me to start teaching classes on the baptism in the Holy Spirit. I love it when the Lord does that.

My struggle with pride is a prime example of how the enemy had planted seeds in my thoughts of "how holy" I had become. When I started walking closer with the Lord and walking in the Spirit, the Lord started revealing things to me and using me to minister to others by the gifts of the Holy Spirit. I think of that verse in James 3:1 that says in essence not to desire to become a teacher knowing that we shall receive a stricter judgement. That makes me tremble.

Isn't it interesting that the Holy Spirit inspired 40 authors to write 66 books and to cover every area of our lives? 2 Corinthians 10:12-13 states that we are not to compare ourselves because it is not wise. Furthermore, it states in verse 13 not to boast beyond measure or more than what God has assigned or appointed to us. So boasting is not good. But if the Lord has used you to touch someone's life in some way and they thank you, learn to say "Thank you" and then thank the Lord. You do not need to say, "Oh that wasn't me, that was God". I would say things like that to make sure God got the glory but I was also saying that out of pride deep inside myself.

When Corrie Ten Boom spoke at our church in the 1970's, she told us something special. When people praise you or thank you just lay that bouquet at the Master's feet giving Him all the glory at the end of your day. When you get those thank-you comments, texts, cards or emails and give them back to the Lord then you won't start lifting yourself up.

Since we are still discussing "bad" things, here's another one. It happens when a person calls themselves a Christian and goes to church on Sunday but the rest of the week they say or do things that are not pleasing to Christ. Making Jesus "Lord" of our life makes the big difference! Oh, how sad, I have heard people tell me that "_____ is a Christian and said he speaks in tongues but he sure doesn't act or talk like a Christian at work". That breaks my heart and that is just more ammunition for the enemy to use against this experience. What about those businesses that use Christian symbols on their sign or business card, yet they do not represent Christ in their work performance, their integrity or their everyday lives?

I keep getting reports from people from time to time who start working for a "Christian business" and end up quitting because the owner doesn't act like a Christian. I had one person tell me he would rather work for a heathen than for a Christian. Oh, how sad. Just because a person is a Christian or has been baptized in the Holy Spirit and speaks in tongues does not make them holier than anyone else, they are still human and God has to work in their life. Even the people in the world know what our lives should be like.

Here's another story right from Acts 15:36-40. Barnabas wanted to take John Mark with him but Paul did not want to because John Mark had deserted them in Pamphylia. They got into quite an argument and the contention was so sharp that they parted from one another, each going their separate ways, on their own missionary journeys. Can you believe two brothers in Christ who have been missionaries together, baptized in the Holy Spirit and even speak in tongues (Paul said he spoke in tongues more than the others) could possibly disagree so much they got into a very heated argument?

Then they took someone else with them on their journey and the Lord used them to minister to more people in other towns. The baptism in the Holy Spirit does not make us perfect or better than others. It makes us better than we were before and helps us in our walk with Christ to share Jesus out of these broken and cracked vessels of clay.

Here's another example from my life of how we can be "Spirit filled and speak in tongues" and yet be totally blind to our flesh and what we do to other people. Here we are "Christians" and still hurting or upsetting people. God will keep working on us if we want Him to and we desire to become more Christ-like.

In 2013, I became aware of something else in my life that was not pleasing to the Lord. I was doing what I thought was good for people even though it was causing more harm. I was not even aware of what I was doing and I thought I was being so helpful. But instead of asking them if they wanted help or what I could do to help them, I would just jump in and start doing "whatever" they were doing and telling them how to do it. I learned that "my good intentions doesn't trump my affects". I started to pray "Lord please bring to the light the things in my life that I am totally blind to and expose them".

Oh yes, the Lord answers prayer! As I shared these things with Barbara she gave me an example to help me understand what I had done years ago. She said that when she was backing out of the driveway I would run out to the middle of the street and make sure it was clear for her and wave for her to come out. I am such a wonderful person and so thoughtful too. She said, "Jerry that really upset me back in those days because I was an adult and I knew how to drive. You meant well and you wanted to help but your good intentions overruled your effects on me, but I never said anything". Really? She had only been driving for 20 years!

Do you understand what I am trying to say? The Lord has brought things to the light that I was not even aware of. The only problem is that it really causes me to resist and react when the Lord uses someone to expose an area in my life that is not Christ-like. Yes, He uses my wife who knows me best and can so easily see when my attitude or thinking or comments are not Christ-like. But I am glad the Lord is still working on me and I thank the Lord for my godly wife! However, she won't cut me any slack!

I have done so many things in my life that have not reflected the heart of God to others even though I have a heart for the Lord. You will always find "Christians" or people who are "baptized in the Holy Spirit and speak in tongues" who have lots of faults. Don't look at Christians just look to Jesus!

The vision of the ladder was meaningful for me! I hope it becomes a guard rail for you in your walk with Christ. The Lord loves us so much and He corrects us in such a gentle way. Lord help me to love others like You do. Matthew 22:35-40 sums it all up when we learn that "LOVE IS THE KEY!"

We can talk in tongues all day, but if we don't have God's love emanating from us, we are like sounding brass or a clanging cymbal as we read in 1 Corinthians 13:1. We can also be used in the gift of prophecy and have amazing faith. However, if we don't have love we are nothing, as is mentioned in verse 2. The day will come when prophecies will fail, tongues will cease and knowledge will vanish away because we will be with Jesus. Verse 13 states *And now abide faith, hope, and love, these three; but the greatest of these is love.* God is the complete definition of love!

The love of God flowing through our life will speak much louder than speaking in tongues. If our life doesn't reflect the true character of Jesus in our words and action then we can bring a bad reflection on Him. The enemy will try to take advantage of every opportunity to shed a bad light on Jesus. So let Jesus shine through in everything you do.

Chapter 12
THE UGLY

Now I want to cover what I refer to as the "ugly" part. What I am referring to are the weird things that I have seen and heard and maybe you have seen or heard in your life time about "charismaniacs" and Pentecostals. These things did not bring glory to the Lord but they sure have brought attention to the people who have said or done these things resulting in the Holy Spirit getting the blame.

When we moved to Arizona in 1952, I remember my mother taking me to many small Pentecostal churches or tent meetings. We visited many different types of "Pentecostal" churches so I got to see and hear a lot of things. Some of it was very emotional and strange and some of it was real.

For example, I heard about people jumping over the bench seats called "pew jumping". I have heard people yelling and screaming so I wondered if they were actually under the power of God. A few times I saw some people rolling around on the floor. No wonder the Pentecostals got the name "Holy Rollers" back in the old days.

I remember doing the "Jericho March" in silence six times around the inside perimeter of the church and I actually enjoyed it. After the seventh time walking around the church we shouted praises to God to bring the walls of the enemy down. That was always fun but I only did that a few times in my life. We were just following the Bible example when Joshua led them around the walls of Jericho, so that was okay and not "weird", but maybe strange if you were a visitor.

Recently a pastor told me that the "freedom in the Spirit" was encouraged in the Pentecostal arena back in the early 1900s, when churches were so rigid and legalistic. People were given total freedom to act and do what they wanted as "they felt the Spirit lead them" and if you stopped or interrupted them you were "quenching the Spirit". I am not saying this information is perfectly accurate, but this is what I was told. It makes more sense now why people were "out of control" and acting from their flesh allowing their emotions to do what they "felt".

Back in the old days I heard of people coming to watch and listen through the windows to see these "holy rollers". Yes there have been a lot of things that have been done, even in recent years and today, that bring attention to the person instead of bringing attention and glory to Jesus. Not only have they come to see it through the window, but they have come into the church to observe the "weird" people. They leave laughing and making fun of the "Pentecostal Christians" or "Charismaniacs". This is just what Satan, who is the enemy of God, wants to do. He wants to discredit anything about God that is real and make fun of anything else he can to scare people away.

Satan will use anything to bring division in churches, families and relationships. He has put fear in people to stay away from the "weird" religious churches and people. It is very unfortunate that he puts them all in one basket even if a church is walking in the Spirit and not weird. If a church believes in the move of the Spirit, the Baptism in the Holy Spirit, speaking in tongues and the gifts of the Spirit, it can get included as one of the weirdo churches.

When I was about 9, my folks invited a new friend to a meeting at a little church in Phoenix. He had been a bronc back rider in South Dakota and had broken bones getting bucked off. His hands were twisted from arthritis and he had been living in a wheelchair for many years. He was prayed for and the Lord healed him. I saw him get out of the wheelchair and he walked. The gifts of healings by the Spirit are mentioned in 1 Corinthians 12:9 and are part of the nine gifts of the Spirit. God is real, He is the healer and I have seen God move in some of those little churches when I was a kid, in spite of the weird stuff. These miracles were not fake then and God is still doing miracles today.

Today on television there have been people "slain in the Spirit", which is when they fall backwards to the floor after the speaker has put their hand on the person's forehead. Is it real or is it fake? Growing up I saw this happen without the pastor touching them. After the service people were gathered up around the front to pray and stand and worship. I saw some fall backwards straight as a telephone pole, hit their head on the wood bench or the concrete floor under the power of the Spirit. We did not have "people catchers" back in those days. After laying there "under the power of the Spirit" for 15-30 minutes that person would get up and not be injured at all.

Does God change? No. Just remember that people get in the "flesh", doing things out of emotions, and can start bringing attention to themselves, whether individuals or pastors or "televangelists". Unfortunately doing things in the flesh is part of the "ugly" that I refer to when it is not of God. However, it could be of God, like when Benny Hinn would pray for people and I was there when he first started his ministry. He just pointed at people and they were "slain in the Spirit". Years later he would blow on them or swing his coat and they would fall backwards "slain in the Spirit". So the Lord was still using him even though his pride was active when he was doing the "weird" stuff. Yes being "slain in the Spirit" is real but it can also be a "pushover".

I was "slain in the Spirit" once so I know it is real. In the 1970s, we were in a small home Bible study group and after the study we were standing in a circle and praying and worshipping the Lord. A friend walked over to me and reached out his hand to touch my head. I floated down backwards straight as a board and softly landed on the floor without my knees buckling. I was not in a trance. I knew what was happening and I felt myself going down. I heard my friends as they knelt down beside me worshipping and praising the Lord. It was like I was in the presence of Jesus under the power of the Spirit and I could not get up. It was such a wonderful time just lying there and worshipping the Lord, crying as the love of Jesus was just saturating me.

After about 30 minutes I sat up. Then I got up and I said, "Val you pushed me". He said, "No Jerry, I didn't even touch you". I argued with him and accused him of pushing me over. He denied it and the others confirmed that his hand never touched me. I said "Thank you Jesus" and I knew it was real. I had been "slain in the Spirit". I was not in a trance.

Since then, I have been pushed over 2 times at various churches that I have visited while traveling and working. I have observed people who have been "slain in the Spirit" go down like a telephone pole, straight as a board. I have also observed others who "I think" wanted to be "slain in the spirit" and their knees buckle and they crumble on the floor. I have seen things on television which make me question what happened. Maybe they were really slain in the Spirit so I have to be careful. I am sure you have seen things on television that are weird or strange or look "fake". It is so sad that these "ugly" things do occur even today.

I recently spoke to a friend on the phone and we were discussing this topic. She voluntarily told me of her experience of being slain in the Spirit and it happened to her just like it did to me. She knew she was going down straight backwards, floating to the floor and landing ever so gently. She knew what was happening around her and heard others praying so she was not in a trance. She felt herself being bathed in the love of Jesus. She also said she has been "pushed over". Just know that this is real and not fake.

When I read in the Bible that someone fell on their face in the Old Testament I believe they went down under the power of the Spirit or in the powerful presence of God and were "slain in the Spirit". In the Gospel of John 18:6 the soldiers in the Garden of Gethsemane drew back and fell on the ground when Jesus said, "I am He". I believe they were overcome by the power of God. Other places in the Bible people "bowed" down which was something I believe they did by choice.

Another thing that I have observed a long time ago and I would put in the class of "ugly" is screaming. It sure did not bring attention to the Lord but it scared me and I am sure it scared the visitors out of their wits. I have seen a person who would stand up and give a blood curdling scream then give the message in tongues. Next, someone in the congregation would give the interpretation of the message in tongues. I believe there was a lack of teaching, a lack of direction and a major lack of correction in the church. The pastor may have felt that he had to allow the "freedom in the Spirit" and not stop what God wanted to in the service.

This was another example of those "ugly" things that I think happen that the enemy will use to scare people away from this experience or away from any church that believes in the gifts of the Spirit and speaking in tongues. He can lie to people and say, "You have to remove your brain if you want to be a Christian or go to that church".

Sometimes when visitors attend a church, things happen that were not condoned by the church leadership. They will do something weird and the church gets branded as "crazy" or "off the deep end", especially when someone used a camera and they put it on social media. How sad, and that is where the enemy comes in to destroy the work of the Spirit and to discredit the name of our Lord and Savior Jesus Christ as well as to that church. You can always read reviews about churches and ministries and get plenty of bad feedback.

Some pastors have taught that "If you are not baptized in the Holy Spirit and speak in tongues you will not go to heaven". That is not in the Bible or the heart of God. If that were true then all of the people of God in the Old Testament will not be in heaven because the Holy Spirit was not poured out until the Day of Pentecost when the 120 spoke in tongues.

I was sharing with a young man about the baptism in the Holy Spirit and he told me that he and his high school friends went to a Pentecostal church just to watch the people. After the service some people came to the back of the church where they were sitting and asked them to come up to the front to be prayed for. The person told my friend and his buddies, "We will teach you how to speak in tongues". He said they ran out of the church. I told him, "I am glad you ran out of that church, we do not teach people how to speak in tongues, that is the work of the Spirit".

In fact, I was on the internet a few years ago and there was a lady who was teaching people how to speak in tongues. Mercy! You do not need anyone to teach you how to speak in tongues.

I could go on and on with more examples of "ugly" things that can happen in the church. It breaks my heart how the enemy has used these events to steal, kill and destroy as we read in John 10:10. He "steals" truth and plant lies, then he "kills" the reputation of the church and Jesus Christ. He wants to "destroy" relationships in families, relatives, friends and churches. But at the end of that verse Jesus *said I have come that they may have life, and that they may have it more abundantly.* Yes, Jesus is the way, the truth and the life! John 10:6.

We still have to be careful because I cannot put God in a box. He may do things in ways that I do not understand. I have found out later that something I felt was not from the Lord proved to be a total God thing! Therefore, I have to search the scriptures, pray, be still and be-quiet.

A perfect example in the Bible is in Acts 3:8, where Peter and John healed the lame man. He went into the temple with Peter and John walking and leaping and praising God. If he came walking and leaping and shouting in church today the ushers would probably usher him out. I certainly would have judged him as "bringing attention to himself instead of the Lord". See how wrong I can be? But God used that incident for Peter to preach and God got the glory!

Do not allow the "weird" things to keep you from seeking more of Jesus. It is an exciting walk with Jesus being led by the Spirit according to Romans 8:14 *For as many as are led by the Spirit of God, these are the sons of God.* According to Galatians 5:18 *But if you are led by the Spirit, you are not under the law.*

In 1 Corinthians 14:32-3 it reads, *And the **spirits of the prophets are subject to the prophets.** For God is not the author of confusion but of peace, as in all the churches of the saints* (emphasis added). What a very important verse! This means that you are in control, you don't have to get weird or do "ugly weird" things. I do not believe that the Holy Spirit will take control of us and make us do something. We can make choices and we don't have to act "out of control" unless we choose to do it.

Remember, there is a difference when the Holy Spirit is leading us or prompting us to do something "weird", like set up a surveillance at 11:00 AM in a city 90 miles away on a Monday. We can learn to know the voice of the Holy Spirit.

This one thing I know from experience and that it is easy to say something or do something that we feel the Lord is directing us because our feelings and emotions are strong. I have done that and realized later that I was acting or speaking out of self, or the "flesh" and it was not the Holy Spirit. The Lord does not hold that against us okay? I feel so bad and I ask the Lord to forgive me. Please don't give up trying to hear the Lord and being obedient to the promptings. We are learning and growing. The Holy Spirit will use you and you will touch lives without being a weird "Charismaniac".

If you visit a church and there is a message in tongues and someone gives the interpretation, just listen to the message. If someone gets up and gives a "word from the Lord" it would probably be a "prophetic word" of edification, exhortation or comfort to the church congregation. In 1 Corinthian chapter

12:1-11 it lists the different gifts of the Spirit including tongues and interpretation of tongues as part of the 9 gifts of the Spirit mentioned there. In Chapter 14, verse 5, Paul writes instruction to the church at Corinth that *I wish you all spoke with tongues, but even more that you prophesied; for he who prophesies is greater than he who speaks with tongues, unless indeed he interprets, that the church may receive edification.*

My word of encouragement here is that when you spend time in the Word and grow in your relationship with Jesus the Holy Spirit will start moving in your life in a greater way. Isn't it wonderful to know that the Holy Spirit is our Helper and He comes along side of us, but He doesn't force us or make us do weird or "ugly" things. He draws us to Jesus and he points everything to the glory of the Father.

CHAPTER 13
TO SUM IT ALL UP

I asked my young friend Jason Schneider about his experience of being baptized in the Holy Spirit and he shared his testimony with me in writing.

As I prayed about it I felt the Lord wanted me to include his testimony as it seems to sum up all the things I have been sharing. Originally I was only going to put in a short paragraph about what he shared but after reading his story I believe you will be blessed and inspired also. I asked his permission and he was happy to let his testimony be included in my book.

Thank you for sharing your life with the world Jason.

"I had been prayed over, for the release of the gift of tongues in my life, as a kid. I remember wanting and asking for it but not having an education behind what I was asking for. I felt the Holy Spirit inside of me in that moment as a kid but the release of the spiritual language did not happen. I was concerned that maybe I wasn't a good enough Christian or had done something that God was possibly angry with me. As a young man I kept all of this information and emotions to myself never reaching out to anyone about the subject. When the gift of tongues was brought up I stayed as far away as possible.

Fast forward... 2016. I'm married with 3 children and answered the call to ministry. Part of this process was attending the Central Valley School of Ministry (CVSOM) founded by John Amstutz in Fresno. One of my courses was the Baptism of the Holy Spirit. This course had 'The Question' I was dreading... "Did you speak in tongues?" I knew Jerry Carlson taught at my church, Valley Christian Center, on the Baptism of the Holy Spirit. Jerry had invested in me as a young man, spent time at men's breakfast meetings and even shot guns with me at the shooting range. He was someone I could confide in and trust to help me answer the question of speaking in tongues.

I called without hesitation and Jerry answered with great enthusiasm as he welcomed me to come to his home. With nerves and emotions from my past experience I stepped into his home. Jerry explained with visual aids (Glasses & Water, Sinners & Believers) what God's Heart was for me. The imparting of this gift is the overflow of the Holy Spirit and its functions within me personally. We stepped into Jerry's backyard where I saw a beautiful log cabin and woods environment. This brought me to my experiences as an outdoorsman in the back country of Montana, a place where I always felt God speak to me through His nature and beauty. So right away I felt peace as Jerry and I took seats inside the log cabin.

Jerry shared his testimony with receiving his gifts and prayed over me. He then led me through a time of being in the presence of God and asked me what I was feeling in that moment. I told him, I felt the Holy Spirit was giving me some words and with Jerry's encouragement and support... I spoke out in my spiritual language! I am eternally grateful Jerry led the way walking me through my fears of the unknown. Isn't this how God operates, He blessed me far and above what I thought might happen! I will always be so fond of my time with the Holy Spirit, my brother in Christ Jerry and his cabin in the woods where I was able to open up and release the gift of speaking in my Spiritual Language.

Thank You Jerry for investing your story and relationship with the Holy Spirit with me. This has brought me into a deeper connection with the Holy Spirit and strengthened the calling I have over my life! I love you very much, thank you for being a brother to me. Jason Schneider"

In Closing

My prayer is that this book will spread like seeds in the wind of the Spirit across the land and water.

My goal was to share what the Lord has shown me and taught me over the years as I investigated this confusing and controversial subject. It will be my joy if people read this book and then share it with others. Also, my prayer is that it will enlighten the reader and draw people into a deeper relationship with Jesus Christ our Lord and Savior.

Again, I am asking you, please don't seek to speak in tongues. Seek to know Jesus more in an intimate way. When you're ready, ask the Lord to baptize you in the Holy Spirit and the spiritual language will come, that is part of the baptism. After you ask, start thanking the Lord and praising Him for baptizing you in the Holy Spirit. You may immediately start speaking in your spiritual language or it may take time. One day you will run out of your own words. At that point your personal prayer and praise language will start to flow out of your inner most being and heart, like rivers of living water, John 7:38-39. There is such joy in this beauty of spiritual language, praying or singing in the Spirit.

I believe that Colossians 3:1-17 summarizes my heart. Get ready for an exciting walk with Jesus as you walk in the Spirit in a new and deeper way.

You can contact me at Jerry.carlson.writer@gmail.com

RECOMMENDED READING AND WATCHING

The Gospel of John

The Book of the Acts of the Apostles

I Corinthians Chapters 12, 13 and 14

Robert Morris, Gateway Church, Southlake, Texas,
How Do I Know?

Robert Morris, Gateway Church, Southlake, Texas.
The God I Never Knew

Mark Cahill, One Heartbeat Away

Mark Cahill, One Thing You Can't do in Heaven

Jimmy Evans, Gateway Church, Southlake, Texas
4 week series on Essential Foundations, June 20, 2020.
https://gatewaypeople.com/series/essential-foundations
Or on YouTube type in "Jimmy Evans Essential Foundations"
https://www.youtube.com/results?search_query=jimmy+evans
+essential+foundations

Jack Deere, Surprised by the Power of the Spirit

Jack Deere, Surprised by the Voice of God

Jack W. Hayford, The Beauty of Spiritual Language: Unveiling
the Mystery of Speaking in Tongues

NOTES

Notes